THE H

C000068245

NOTE

Sounding Love in Your Life
from Your Heart's Secret Chamber

FINDHORN PRESS

Also by Stewart Pearce

BOOK

The Alchemy of Voice

SET OF CARDS

Angels of Atlantis Oracle Cards

CDS/MP3S

The Alchemy of Voice - Awakening
The Alchemy of Voice - Initiation
Sonic Meditations

BOOK, SET OF CARDS AND MP3S
AVAILABLE FROM
www.findhornpress.com

CDS AVAILABLE FROM
www.thealchemyofvoice.com

THE HEART'S NOTE

Sounding Love in Your Life
from Your Heart's Secret Chamber

STEWART PEARCE

FINDHORN PRESS

Published in 2010 by Findhorn Press, Scotland

ISBN 978-1-84409-506-3

Edited by Michael Hawkins and Ellen Gunter
Front cover design by Richard Crookes
Interior by Damian Keenan
Printed and bound in the European Union

1 2 3 4 5 6 7 8 9 17 16 15 14 13 12 11 10

Published by
Findhorn Press
117-121 High Street,
Forres IV36 1AB,
Scotland, UK

t +44 (0)1309 690582
f +44 (0)131 777 2711
e info@findhornpress.com
www.findhornpress.com

Acknowledgments

Writing a book can literally consume your life, and from the deeper recesses of my Heart's Secret Chamber I thank my dear ones, like Reza, who kept me balanced through their love of laughter, as I grappled with the words that poured from me, in a vain attempt to decide if they were chosen as the best.

I've tried steadfastly to write as though speaking, so that all who read may hear, so that all who peruse may feel with their finer sense, so that all who flow with these thoughts may breathe the rhythm of feeling. For what else is there?

I've spent more than fifty years consciously engaged in the beauty, lustre and thrill of speaking, and I'm honoured that the Angels and the great Alchemy Master have inspired me to bring these words through from the Source, as though from the great Sound Field itself.

Profound gratitude must go to Thierry Bogliolo, and all at Findhorn Press for their loving guidance, and their extraordinary support for the ideas expressed in this writing.

The deepest love and admiration resound towards my glamorous, wonderful Literary Agent, Kay McCauley, without whose presence and support, life would appear rather bleak.

Similarly, thanks go to Michael Hawkins for his editorial care, as he repeatedly reminded me of over-writing, and gently mollified my author's nervousness, whilst concerned with simplifying the concepts wrapped in the many 'notes' or words, that seemingly poured forth as though from Orpheus' magic Lute. Whatever may shine in this book is as a result of his craft and patience. Whatever may be tarnished is because of me.

Thanks go to Ellen Gunter as second editor.

Heartfelt blessings go to Richard Crookes, my wonderful illustrator, who gave such beauty to this book cover and also to 'The Alchemy of Voice'. May our co-creativity grow with the aid of the Angels, and unfold more fully through the future of the Oracle.

Finally, such love and gratitude must go to those wonderful beings all over the Globe who have passed through the portal of the temple of sound healing known as The Alchemy Of Voice. All have taught and enchanted me to think and feel in ways that have stretched my psyche throughout the vistas of eternity. This book is dedicated to you.

Stewart Pearce,
October 2010

Contents

PROLOGUE

Your vision will only become clear when you look into your heart.
Who looks outside, dreams. Who looks inside, awakens.

~ *CARL JUNG*

This is a truly amazing time to be alive. Yet this is also a critical period in all our lives. Huge philosophical, political, societal, economic and planetary changes gnaw at the very bones of our lives, demanding that we stretch our skin and go not without but within, to the very core of our being. When we move to this centre, we find a heart not drowsy but similarly alert to the possibility of unique change, burning with the flame of love, yearning to speak its own purpose, desiring to sound the very song of the soul.

For it is only by awakening your heart, by experiencing how it entrains the whole of your consciousness, remembering that it holds within its very centre your divine blueprint, that you may speak the utter truth of your liberation. This truth, radiant with pure love and joy, will allow you to fully incarnate and therefore to totally embody the fullness of life. This degree of love makes us more available to serve our brothers and sisters, and therefore to nobly enhance planetary evolution.

The heart symbolises life on planet Earth, and as such is a three dimensional organ, moving in three directions within a spiral. Metaphysically, through the heart the blood flows in a figure of eight, the symbol of infinity. Furthermore, within its core lies a secret chamber whose very walls reverberate with the eternal jewels of love, empathy and compassion. These gems are ancient in their stored wisdom, and stir the presence of infinity within. They evoke through their teaching our ability to heal our lives, and consequently to heal our world. Through their overt use we live the probability, and not just the possibility, of co-creating intelligent new paradigms with astonishing authenticity. For we are on the brink of a gargantuan breakthrough in human consciousness, steered not by ourselves but by God's love and will – the creative intelligence that rests at the centre of all cosmic life, which is consciousness itself.

God's Wake-Up Call

God's wake up call for Planet Earth rings out on the Winter Solstice of December 21st, 2012 – a date that contains a unique astrological configuration, recorded two millennia ago by the ancient Mayan and Aztec calendars. As this cosmic alarm bell awakens us from cycles of nature that exist in the profundity of recorded time, the 2,500-year-long life of the Piscean Age finalises, and our lives become wilfully stirred by the dawning of the Aquarian Age. This new epoch will activate within us co-creative energies that help us bring about a Golden Age of unprecedented proportion.

Prophetic statements from the Aztec, Hopi and Mayan people, as well as from historic individuals such as Nostradamus, Dr. John Dee and Edgar Cayce, have foretold this time of great change. All have indicated that a period at the end of the twentieth century and the beginning of the twenty-first century would host colossal change. These powers believed that transformation would regenerate a profound understanding, concerning our creative integration within the soul of the Universe.

Furthermore, ancient Mayan Astronomers recorded that the Sun would synchronize with the centre of the galaxy on 21.12.2012, as it does every 26,000 years (known as the precession of the equinoxes). At this point in time, the Sun will receive a spark of light from energy clustered in the Universe, causing it to shine more intensely, and to produce changes within the magnetic field of the galaxy. Occurring thus, Planet Earth will receive an impulse of love of unprecedented proportion, from the very centre of the galaxy.

The possibility exists that this may cause a wobbling of the Earth's axis that literally alters the Planet's orientation, and which will open a portal for a huge influx of light, directed at Planet Earth from the heart of the galaxy, for the closer we are to our galaxy's centre, the greater the *enlightenment*. Such a phenomenon heralds a re-birth, an offering to humanity to assimilate something far richer and more whole than ever before. It is a remarkable time to be alive on the Blue Planet.

My belief is that our lives will be vastly transformed, providing an opportunity from which the fear-based culture of the Piscean Age shifts to a much higher vibration, based on the harmony of love. And so be it. As we reach the culmination of thousands of years of evolution, we may be the first civilization of human beings to radically change the direction of our planet's evolution, through our conscious awareness of choice.

Since before the Industrial Revolution, we have perpetrated acts of gross foolishness disregarding the nature of our planetary home, by desacralizing Mother Earth. We have forgotten that in one pinch of soil there are more precious microbes than are people on our planet. Preoccupied with mass consumerism, pollution levels have soared, affecting the very breath of our planet's future life. Profoundly, the energy accumulations that determine the very effluent of our material greed threaten us with global warming.

A Time Of Renaissance

All these facts and more charge us to change, to develop newer faculties. We must acquire radical evolutionary management skills, to produce a level of responsibility and a maturity of wisdom that are informed by our deepening and divinely inspired emotional intelligence. You see, our hearts will be called to open their temple doors and to allow their virtuous content to soar with the power of compassion that supersedes any other virtue – compassion acts as a key to that which endures, a passion that knows love to be the only crucible through which we can truly survive. Thus we find a way to optimize our creative potential, full of the ecstasy of sustained joy.

As we pass through this portal, each of us has the opportunity to unfold, to evolve, to maximize the potential of God's plan, and not just through the action of *science*. Knowing science means we understand the conditions of life, but then as we move through this era of qualitative growth and name our heart's passion, we will understand the extent to which we must surrender the thoughts of science to another plan. Fatefully, this neo-paradigm establishes the truth-filled efficacy of our role in creation, for it brings us to know our *conscience* as a means to access the probability of the afterlife.

Our primary role is beauty itself incarnate: that we open our hearts to the highest choice that we ourselves can possibly create. It is through the expression of joy that we utterly deduce what we want to be, as divine beings in human form, and through the conscious living of divinely inspired emotional intelligence, we stop the conspiracy of sabotaging our natural talents, living in fear and only doing what other people want us to do. For the challenge has always been to be oneself in a world that is trying to make one like everybody else.

At this time, I believe we are summoned to open our hearts in a special way, and in order to do this, we must release the subtlety of the Ego. We must bravely negotiate the confines of our negative thoughts and fears, which ultimately force a depletion of our power. We must work hard, through excavating our interior lives, through spiritual exercise to heal the pain that brims from our shadow, and from life, for life is the gymnasium of the Soul.

The Power of Magic In Life

Immersed in technology, and yet ravished by our need for the soul of the sacred, we seek the landscape of the inspired epic. These great stories alert our imagination, summoning it to salve our lives by drenching us in the knowledge and wisdom of timeless stories. The consequential and essential elements of our mythic or archetypal consciousness open before us: dazzling, evocative, wrenching and powerfully educative.

Hence the universal popularity of magical films like *The Lord of the Rings, Harry Potter* and *Avatar* – which not only bring back the magic that has been missing from storytelling for centuries, they also restore our hope in the belief that all is not lost for our planet. They restore our lives through the exquisite prophecy that life is sustainable. Their fascination and spectacle are overwhelming. Their ravishing substance portrays the only form worth breathing for – loving truth made fully manifest and totally believable.

Through distrust in the dogma of our religious hierarchies, we turn to imagination to balance our morality. For the archetypal field of imagination is where the light rests clearly, shoulder to shoulder with the dark, the masculine and feminine, the constrictions and freedoms – our progressions and our dwindling constitutions all rest as one. The mythic archetypes of our epic stories provide us with powerful keys to our consciousness, enabling us to develop and sustain the deeper aspect of our nature when everything else begins to fall away. As Hamlet says: *"This above all: to thine ownself be true. For there is nothing either good or bad, that thinking makes it so."*

Living Our True Sovereignty

If we can be inspired to live better lives, we may be liberated to the conviction of our true sovereignty, that being our divinity. This optimized potential means we connect with the vision of the most spiritual of teachings, as we become instruments of *Love.*

When our hearts are closed to *Love* we are not ourselves; we are merely hostages to the Ego. Whereas when we function as hosts to God, our optimizing, our unfolding, our purpose, all point in the same direction, focusing us in a peace-filled inner balance. This free breath, this pure pulse, this cosmic flow, this restored balance brings love to the sanctity of each moment.

The Sacred Language Of The Past

Much before the astronomical cycle of the past 5,125 years, human beings used a form of language completely unlike the present. This language was of the heart. As ancient as the rocks and wind, this mode of communication created a fusion between mind and body, a coherence of both right and left brain hemispheres, and a knowledge of thought and feeling as one. The transmission centre was the secret chamber of the heart known as the **Shante Ishta**, the single eye of the heart.

Indigenous peoples, such as the Mayan, the Aztec and the Kogi still believe the secret chamber of the heart to be the core of all that is sacred about life. Indeed, it is recorded in the book of Genesis, that in ancient times all people of the Earth knew one language, until humanity defied God by building the great Tower of Babel – *'making their names to be scored upon heaven'*.

God's infinite wisdom responded by dispersing all nations, by separating all people in order to confound their intention. From thence the soul became individualized, and egoist tendencies inflated the notion of separation from the *Source*. The life of heart-felt communion became isolated in each person, until this time.

The Secret Chamber Of The Heart

The secret chamber of the human heart is where the individual soul attunes to the collective, universal heartbeat, that unites us all through a vast field of intention — that of consciousness. When we choose to love from our heart we enter into a chamber of creation where all things meet in genesis, the legendary 'gene of Isis', for it is from the Great Mother Isis, the formative energy of the primordial silence, that all life originally arose. And so the truth of creation unfolded and still unfolds.

There is an ancient legend of the magical Isis, who was the Goddess of Fertility in the myths of ancient Egypt. Isis was the daughter of Geb, the God of the Earth, and Nut, the Goddess of the overarching sky. Isis, story suggests that her husband, Osiris, had been cruelly killed by the jealous Set, and his dismembered body parts, thirteen in all, had been strewn about the Earth. However, Isis found and brought together twelve of the parts, excepting Osiris's penis; this she fashioned anew from gold, and sang a song of such exquisite beauty that Osiris was resurrected from death, and became the Lord of the Afterlife.

If we can follow the example of Isis, taking her song of creation and once more singing our own song, speaking the language of our hearts from the secret chamber of the heart, we may truly become a vessel for the embodiment of love. Then ingratitude, judgement, hatred, lack of compassion, or refusing to forgive cease to exist - for to be anything other than love is to be without soul.

The New Song Of Creation

Our power to love is the surrendering of our separate sense of self to the inclusivity of life, to life as a collective force. When we claim the right to be a total part of this living, we enjoy a seismic shift of consciousness. We cease being an individual in the sense of recognizing our identity as separate, and we become part of the transparency and inclusivity of the Source, of universal force. Thence an old song is made new.

This song stimulates 'connectivity', and inspires the creativity that is within the infinite field of possibility – the knowledge of Divine Love as the fruit of the *source*. Once we connect, we exchange our mortal intelligence with that of divine wisdom, and nothing is the same again. We embark on a voyage of the miraculous, and time as an agent of infinity expands, allowing creative action to follow the purest of paths.

Life foretells it is impossible to act for self, alone, when knowing self means to know God within. To act any other way is to destroy the nature of our life, which is fused by God's breath. The ancients knew this as the anima mundi, the pranayama, the animating principle of the universe. This inclusive part of God's plan means knowing all souls, for if someone suffers somewhere in the world, their suffering is felt locally. When the critical mass of humanity realizes this, there will be a radical shift, and conflict in the form of war will simply cease to exist.

Living A Model Of Love

When we live life in right minded-ness, we all want a world modelled in God's image, the fulfilment of love. As we move into this right mind, the world becomes a place where the cry of the child is comforted, where the anguish of the sick at heart is heard, where truth is not denied, where the pain of the fallen is healed, where the bloodshed ceases, and where all people feel their joyous ability to live a path of celestial conduct — honestly, heartily, humbly and wholly. Our objective must be to create this world in which lovelessness is simply not an option. Our vision must be to create a world where such things as war are literally unthinkable. Our legacy must be to love a world into creation, that is formed by the miraculous for the miraculous, a world where each person will feel inspired to spend many moments of each day feeling love for the whole of creation.

This is the time for opening the heart's chamber, an occasion when our heart's voice rhythmically yearns for us to creatively speak loving action. This is a period when we must recognize that time is a rhythmic cycle of life. A time that allows us to see our well-being in delicate balance, and our hearts as the central force that stabilizes the rhythm of our bodies.

The Power Of The Heart

Science reveals that a human foetus's heart begins beating before the brain is formed. This 'auto-rhythm' suggests the heart to have a self-initiated beat, which precedes conscious thought, dispelling the illusion of the brain's intellectual function as the foremost principle in the creation of human life - the heart's beating is the elixir that enervates human consciousness.

The heart has its own independent nervous system with 40,000 neurons, as many as are found in the sub-cortex of the brain. Scientific experimentation at the Fels Institute for Cancer Research and Molecular Biology in Philadelphia discovered that when the brain sends orders to the heart, the heart doesn't obey. Instead, the heart appears to be sending messages back to the brain, and the brain not only understands it obeys.

It must be our utmost conviction to allow the power of our hearts to manage our thoughts and feelings, to live to the heartbeat of emotional truth. As we consciously move to the beat of this drum, transformation reveals a bridge between linear thinking and intuitive sensing. This landscape alone provides us with both a greater perception, and a way of creating solutions to face future complexity with greater ease.

We must stop the frenzy of our stress-filled living, fulfilling functions that simply create disease. We must stop the actions that lead to the closing of the heart, and the explosions of the heart in the form of cardiac arrest.

The Gateway To Unity

Instead, we must start listening to our heart, sensing with our heart, thinking with our heart, feeling with our heart, choosing with our heart, meditating with our heart, and speaking from our heart. We must realize the profound limits in just placing blind faith in the paradigms and systems of science alone. We must develop visionary faith at this time, knowing that something more is needed for the fulfilment of human nature and its spirit.

More than ever, as we meet the challenges of the twenty-first century — the fear of terrorism, of soaring productivity, of breathtaking instantaneity, and the advantages of living in a global village with ever decreasing borders created by information technology — people can see the possibility of a merger between science and spirit. Lamentably, what co-exists with this is our ability to wreak havoc on our planet through nuclear warfare, genetic engineering and global warming.

Let us remember that the heart is a gateway for unification. The heart links us to a higher intelligence, drawing together both thought and feeling, opening us to a kingdom of the intuition, the domain of the imagination, where the divine and mundane meet in an ecstasy of finer feeling. Saint-Exupery wrote: *"Now here is my secret, a very simple secret; it is only within the heart that one can see rightly; what is essential is invisible to the naked eye."*

However, the heart is not a sentimental organ; it is forthright, brave and substantial. It supports and nourishes all systems of the body during a life-long commitment to excellence. Moreover, the intelligence of the heart has within it a power that signals the next level of development within the survival of our species.

We must shout "enough!" to the conviction of hatred, and strike open the conviction of love. We must shout "enough!" to the belief that the fortitude of the terrorist is greater than the sustenance of the lover. This is simply not the case in a heaven where such action does not exist. The attention placed on terrorism in each moment of today's media is palpable. This simply must cease.

Similarly, we must cultivate a peaceful earth where decisions about going to war, to vanquish a nation that poses a threat, simply do not exist. As Albert Einstein once said: *"The significant problems we face today cannot be solved at the same level of thinking we were at when we created them."*

Our task is to free ourselves from the tyranny of our ego, from the prison of our false belief in the illusion of exclusivity. By widening our field of compassion, and embracing the whole of life in its beauty, we experience ecstasy. Through the empathy of our physical, emotional, mental and spiritual integration, we at last shuffle off the manacles of despair that have held us in so tight a grip.

> *"My heart is so small*
> *it's almost invisible.*
> *How can You place*
> *such big sorrows in it?"*
> *"Look", He answered,*
> *"your eyes are even smaller,*
> *yet they behold the whole world."*
>
> *~ RUMI*

The Heart's Intelligence

Current belief states that the heart's intelligence has a flow of awareness and insight brought about as we consciously develop our personal power through initiation after initiation – *the thousand natural shocks that flesh is heir to.* The heart gives us emotional and intuitive data that helps us govern our lives. The heart always knows best through the highest choice, whereas the head indecisively chatters: *"Shall I shan't I, will I won't I?"*

Once thought and feeling have been brought into balance, we reach a rich form of super-coherence, a way of perceiving that unveils our truest magic. As William Blake wrote: *"When the doors of our perception are opened, we see life truly as it is, limitless."*

Today's human potential movement, the wisdom culture of tomorrow, explores how we can open our minds to a sense of infinity, to a level of awareness without the shock of societal trauma like the destruction of the World Trade Centre in 2001, the Tsunami of 2004 or the horrors of hurricane Katrina in 2005. Albeit, these cataclysms were a form of initiation that opened our hearts to compassion for those who perished or suffered!

A Vision of Infinity

The vision that startles our heart conjures those personal moments of inspiration that completely alter our lives. Those occasions are the awakenings that arise from a place of great stillness, and yet in their ordinariness, have vast landscapes within them that open us to the mystery of life. Thus we transform how we learn through desperation into inspiration.

Occasions where an avalanche of group feeling brings about a divine arousal, a deep soul tingle in our DNA, and moves us in a nanosecond from Homo Sapiens into Homo Noeticus, from intelligence into wisdom, for:

"Never doubt that a small group of thoughtful,
committed citizens can change the world.
Indeed, it is the only thing that ever has."
- *MARGARET MEAD*

As I process these thoughts in the autumn of 2010, I'm reminded of those global events that carved out our immediate history in the twentieth century, and that had a profound effect on all of us, because they aroused our compassion. One example is the death of JFK in 1963, whose assassination proved to be a traumatic moment in U.S. history, and which had a defining impact on the whole nation.

Another was the metaphoric and literal event of the Berlin Wall falling in 1989, which brought light to the shadow-lands of the oppressive Patriarchy richly curdled in the cup of totalitarianism. This was a remarkable movement in the direction of observable collective freedom, and was preceded by Mikhail Gorbachev imparting to Ronald Reagan: *"I'm going to do something terrible to you; I'm going to take away your enemy."*

The spy came in from the cold and warmed himself by the fires of freedom, and the 'cold war' collapsed.

Global Incoherence

Lamentably, the super-power of the western governments immediately created another spectre, that of the Islamic terrorist. The creation of the shadow gave vent to the dread we had all feared, of evil perpetrating evil.

Conversely, contemporary neo-science quantifies the universe from a holographic perspective, substantiating that all we see without is a mirror image of that we create within. It took the mythic personality of the Huntress in the form of Princess Diana to ignite the fire of the collective consciousness. Her bizarre death in August 1997 flowed through us as though we were instruments in some greater drama. Diana, like Artemis, awakened the archetypal force which created spontaneity far beyond our personal ability to emotionally release, and which became the conduit that centred millions of people in wholeness. Diana's death lamentations were the metaphor for the un-realized potential within the core Feminine aspect of our collective being.

Then, the absolute horror of watching two airplanes fly into the twin towers of the World Trade Centre on September 11th, 2001, is another of these events. Those who were in fear of their lives being taken by the noxious fumes of the burning carnage, literally hurled their bodies into space from the towers where they worked. They knew that this sacrifice, this final pledge to life itself would be fatal, but still they jumped. What utter courage moved these people to the belief that something might just happen to intercede, to allow them to continue in flesh to love life, to love their dear ones.

I find it almost impossible to conceive the events that took place that day, even though my eyes were fixed for seven hours to a TV screen, from the very first moment I heard what had happened. All thoughts move not to the literal horror, although one somehow honours the solemnity of its rite, but more to what the event meant in terms of our spiritual intelligence. And I believe that each person who died on September 11th had made an agreement at soul level to be a volunteer in the substance of global transformation.

Global Coherence

The events of 9/11 released a tidal wave that swept through our lives, disturbing that, that is already filled with antitheses. Ah, but the wise will say the contrasts, the diversity of the paradox, keeps us growing. Indeed, if duality ceases to be within or without us, energy becomes calcified. If we balance these forces at the still point, at the centre of the tension between the opposites, our hearts are struck open by a love that is greater than anything we have known before.

The key to our new future lies in us working together, with our hearts vibrant in unity consciousness. Therefore, we must turn to the verity of the heart's impulse: seeing, feeling all that exists within the pulse of each moment's promise, and so we may qualify our truth by living the transparency of the soul.

To conclude, this book aims to give you effective and easy-to-follow exercises for living in the secret chamber of the heart; for making life choices by 'heart dowsing'; for healing our bodies through 'heart sounding'; for committing to a higher purpose through 'heart sacraments'; for seeing what part each of us has in God's plan to heal the world through 'heart empathy'; for developing strategies of 'weighing the heart' for greater integrity;

for using 'heart forgiveness' as a talisman for peace; for calling on the loving guidance of the Archangelic realms; for discerning how the 'devotional pathway of the heart' can bring well-being, and to create miracles in our daily lives.

When we live in this chamber of creation, we create the probability of true transcendence using the core tools of gratitude, non-judgement and forgiveness.

The knowledge contained within this book will help you to step on the path of happiness and devotion. Each reader will I hope feel uplifted, because this book, like the heart, exists through its own auto-rhythm, and produces vibrations that hugely affect the very physical fibre of our lives.

So let us begin.

CHAPTER ONE

The Heart And The Feather

*It's easy to believe in love when you're surrounded by kindness;
it's not so easy when you are confronted by the judgments
and attacks of the world.*

- MARIANNE WILLIAMSON

We are presently living through a time that will come to be known as a time of reckoning. A time when the conscience of the heart will be weighed against the weight of a feather, for the feather in ancient times was seen as an instrument of truth. This is an era when all will witness personal and collective growth beyond measure. An epoch where the endeavour of human truth will ultimately be put to test by uncompromising change, and all illusions will be purified by transparency.

As we move through this rite of passage, our essence will be recalibrated by powerful celestial forces; we will make an evolutionary choice to create life consciously rather than living an unconscious, automatic pilot existence. Indeed, we can already feel planetary forces working through us to determine that wisdom be wrought from the rugged experience of feeling. When we vibrate a truth that permeates through the whole of our physical beings, we experience an integrated flow of force surging through our hearts and filled with the fullness of love and joy. Thence our hearts overflow with compassion, mercy and grace, and sound integrity from the fullest conviction, formed simply by the glory of our love.

Purification

However, before this occurs, there is purification to be made. The golden imperative of cleansing, as an ordained ritual, will wash through our hearts, removing the power to hate or despair, healing us by the love of the divine. For, before we become as human angels full of counter-gravitational force and suffused with the light of love, we must identify a pathway of devotion, and acknowledge it to be one of observation, discipline, liberation and transcendence.

Deep down the desire to transcend is inherent in all of us. A force that only passes us by if the portal of our heart is closed. If our hearts are not open, the planet appears a harsh place with few miracles occurring, until finally we reach out and eventually surrender to grace. For, *"No pessimist ever discovered the secrets of the stars, or sailed to an uncharted land, or opened a new heaven to the human spirit,"* wrote Helen Keller.

As we move through this period of transition, we can observe within our collective societies the need for the shadow to be cleansed. As day follows night and night day, the simplicity of truth speaks out, that light will shine on darkness, revealing much of the anguish in our souls. We all know too well the power of fear in our lives, and how we avoid its cure by a fear of change, pushing it further away. This means we squeeze it into the deeper recesses of our unconscious mind, until it re-appears with doubled strength, exuding its toxic confusion into our lives.

To understand this notion more fully, review our current world and the excesses of reality TV, in particular the opening of the psychic underworld through the 'shadow policeman' reflected in the TV reality show *Big Brother*.

Furthermore, observe the voracious activities of the media, penetrating people's lives with the cold, inscrutable eye of the camera. Watch the rabid litigation searing through the varying constructs of the 'Establishment', all in response to corporate corruption, personal greed and political incorrectness. See the diminishment of social boundaries that once determined social class, observe the toxic pollution that decrees death to many of our planet's most treasured species, the violent competition, the acts of brash exclusivity, continued depletion of earth's resources, and the growing contribution to greenhouse gases.

All and more are the expressions of the Ego, the explosions of the shadow-land of the unconscious. Like a scalpel through skin, these pollutions expose the very tissue of the body politic, to find an organ beneath that has been hidden by a power that disdains; this organ is the heart.

Like a beautiful prism, forged in the most especial of Crystal Caves, the heart will shine forth its truth; for when truth emerges from the energy of the heart, God is ignited within. Yet, before we experience the richness of this, archaic paradigms associated with the supremacy of patriarchal power need to be removed, and then the love of power is transmuted into the power of love. For it is rightfully time to remove the hypocrisies of our Leaders who have hidden behind the smoke screen of their control dramas, haranguing rhetoric, political skirmishes and perpetrations based on status alone. All will be 'outed', whilst the humble and pure of heart will triumph, and the crooked will be made straight.

The Heart's Supremacy

In times of severe chastening, on occasions of great change, in moments of terrible darkness, we often feel lost, and so we turn to the pinnacle points of truth - the eternal compasses, that we know provide us with succour, clarity and aid. Often these verities reside within us, as memories of inspirational moments, or the love that we once received from our Mothers and Lovers. Then, often when we are distanced from our source, and in profound confusion, we seek the elixir of poetry which reminds us of whom we truly are, for:

"When power leads man toward arrogance,
poetry reminds him of his limitations.
When power narrows the areas of man's concern,
poetry reminds him of the richness and diversity of his existence.
When power corrupts, poetry cleanses,
for art establishes the basic truths which must serve
as the touchstones of our judgment."
- JFK OCTOBER 26TH, 1963

Throughout the centuries, philosophers, artists and poets have regarded the heart's elixir to be at the centre of life – for when people speak with sincerity they speak from the heart, when we fall into despair we are disheartened, when we feel our hearts are broken or contorted by betrayal we flounder. Then the heart as the seat of the soul, whose ultimate act is compassion, produces the cure that connects our humanity with the divine.

Many ancient cultures maintained that the prime function of the heart was to direct and influence our emotions for honest decision making, for probing morality, and for celestial celebration: a wise statesman, Agrippa Agricola in ancient Rome, said: *"The heart influences the understanding and gauges all thought, for this produces the wisdom of the sages."*

The Heart Of Significant Cultures

Deep in the Mayan civilization lies an ancient belief that the heart is synonymous with the metaphor of poetic thought, for poetry expresses a distillation of feeling emerging from the deep fissures within the human soul.

An anonymous Dominican friar working in Mexico in the late 1590s compiled a dictionary of 10,000 Spanish words and their Tzotzil (the language of the Mayan) equivalents. He recorded more than 80 metaphors, which refer to the heart as a testament of the Mayans' deep reverence for what they believe to be the locus of all that is significant in the life of the human being. Repentance, for example, is expressed in five different Tzotzil metaphors: *"my heart cries," "my heart grows small," "my heart hurts," "my heart withdraws," and "my heart becomes two."*

Similarly, in the world's great religions of Buddhism, Hinduism, Islam, Jewish and Christian traditions the heart guides and surpasses all other faculties:

"For as a man thinketh in his heart, so is he."

~ OLD TESTAMENT PROVERBS, 23:7

In Tibetan Buddhist and traditional Chinese medicine, the heart is seen as a central passageway between the mind of thought and the body of sensation. The heart is believed to hold 'shen' (which in English translates as both spirit and mind), and flows through the meridian lines of the body as 'chi' or life force - so the arteries carry the nature of life within them. Furthermore, Chinese doctors believe they can perceive harmony imbalance within each organ, purely from the pulse of the heart, and so the Chinese written characters for: 'thought', 'virtue', 'love' and 'intent' all include the character signifying the heart.

Just so, Rabbinical Judaism has within its heart an esoteric doctrine known as Kabbalah, and in recent years these profound spiritual practices have been made a vogue by the pop singer Madonna. Kabbalists use a central practice meditating on the Tree of Life, as a model of human reality depicting a 'map of creation'. This consists of ten energy centres known as Sephirot, at the core of which is the 'heart' connecting all of the centres together. This is known as the *Tifferet,* which in translation means 'beauty and harmony'. And so we see Kabbala teaching from the heart's balance, from which we ultimately experience grace.

Similarly, in Ancient Egypt there existed a profound belief that the heart was a place of balance, and a centre for a life of justness: a place from which all of life's actions could be remembered. No thought, word or deed could be disregarded, for the truth of each incarnation was believed to be a programme of progressive development leading to the next incarnation.

Egyptian Book Of The Dead

The ancient Egyptian death process was considered to be a crucial part of knowing the heart, of 'telling the truth', and so they conducted the deceased through the greatest of test. The Egyptian *Book of the Dead* reveals a ritual in which the Jackal God of Death, Anubis, took the dead person

24

before the great scales of justice in the Hall of Truth. Anubis then placed the heart of the deceased on the left tray of the scales of justice, whilst the feather of Maat, the Goddess of Truth & Justice, was placed on the right tray. If the heart of the deceased outweighed the feather, it was decided that the heart was full of evil deeds. In this event, Ammut, a God with a crocodile's head, hippopotamus legs and the body of a lion devoured the heart, and condemned the deceased to eternal oblivion.

However, if the heart was lighter than the feather, it was recorded that the deceased had led a righteous life, and could be presented before the God King Osiris, to *wholeheartedly* join the afterlife. Thoth, the ibis-headed God of Wisdom stood at the ready, observing all as a record.

"O heart of my being!
Do not rise up against me as witness,
Do not oppose me in the tribunal,
Do not rebel against me before the guardian of the scales!
You are my KA (soul) within my body
Go to the good place prepared for us.
Do not make my name stink before
The magistrates who put people in their places!
If it's good for us, it's good for the judge,
For it pleases him who renders judgment.
Do not invent lies before the god,
Before the great god, the Lord of the west.
Lo, your uprightness brings vindication."
FROM THE EGYPTIAN BOOK OF THE DEAD

Being In The Hall Of Truth

This material illuminates the means by which our own position in life may be called into question: to face the truth that is inevitable and inescapable. For in times such as this era of reckoning, the scales of truth weigh the integrity of our being, allowing a clarity to appear, that moves us forward in the ritual of our own dying; for within each moment of each breath is the glory of our death, and a return to the *source*.

Terence McKenna, the visionary Ethno-botanist said before his death, *"We are on the brink of possibilities that will make us literally unrecognizable to ourselves. These possibilities will be realized not in the next two and a half thousand years, but within the next twenty, because the acceleration of invention and novelty and information transfer is at this point rapid."*

Later in this writing I've compiled a list of questions as witness to the truth about our heart. Answering these points or others like them is vital for the transparency of where we feel ourselves to be — in the reckoning of our veracity. For your heartfelt answers will indicate some of the key personal qualities exacted by your life's path.

Isn't it true that when our integrity is unseen or feels incoherent, when we truly wish to heal, when we are bewildered by confusion, when we weep at losing ourselves and the path to our very soul, when the pain reaches fever pitch, when our life is threatened, we ask for strategies to help us become more aware of that which stops us from being whom we truly are, fully integrated and full of Joy. For make no mistake, *Love* and *Joy* are our birthright; all else is simply an illusion!

The Weighing Of The Heart Test

These questions are substantive ways of considering the actions of your heart, of becoming more creatively within the heart of 'NOW':

1. Do you feel that your heart is heavy with burden?
2. Do you feel that your heart is alight with life?
3. How often do you act compassionately to yourself?
4. How often do you act compassionately to others?
5. Have you consciously eliminated defensive anger from your life?
6. Are appreciation and gratitude keys to your living?
7. Do you make life choices with your heart?
8. Are you sentimental in the use of your heart?
9. Do you love to give and receive in your life?
10. What work do you engage in to alleviate the suffering of others?
11. Are you lovingly healing the 'Heart Stabs' of life?
12. Do you consciously celebrate the 'Heart Tingles' of life?

As you evaluate these questions, they will bring powerful awareness to your heart. Therefore, make conscious choices about bringing the strategy of heartfelt action (in doing and being/giving and receiving) into each moment of each day. *All this requires is the sole belief that love exists as a central premise within the presence of the Cosmos.*

In effect, this means living life fully in your heart, making each choice with the heart — that is every choice — and by so doing being present to the sanctity of each moment. You see when we stop to consider the NOW we realize how fast we have been moving, attempting to accomplish the multitudinous tasks that ridiculously fill our daily lives.

Would you agree that you spend too much of your time rushing around, in an attempt to achieve that which fixates you about the immediate future, rather than being present to each moment of the now-ness of now? What is the point of the zillions of overly controlled goals? During the daily life of most human beings, approximately 60,000 thoughts occur. Social scientists suggest that 50,000 of these thoughts concern goals that we haven't achieved, through energy spent in negative feeling. If we truly recognize that *Thought Creates Reality*, and *Feeling Manifests Actuality*, what sort of world are we creating with fifty thousand thoughts a day that hold negativity and inaccuracy?

To help with becoming more enfolded within the NOW of your heart's secret chamber, after each of the expositions below, I have included a Mantra to create powerful vibrations throughout the whole of your consciousness; from the heart that you know is ready for recalibration.

When we avow and align with the magic of NOW, we live life fully in respect of:

• Living lovingly and compassionately for all Life
• Being a guardian of the Planet
• Protecting the sanctity of creation in all living things.

STRATEGY ONE:
Do you feel your heart is heavy with burden?

If your heart feels heavy, what is it that weighs you down? What size is your burden? What would it feel like if you released the burden?

Consider the condition as closely as you can, discuss the situation with someone whom you trust. Find ways of clearing and purifying the holding in your heart.

Remember, when we are called to consciousness, when we see the interconnectivity of all living things, and before we shift to higher octaves of harmony, we often hit zero. Inevitably, this may make us feel heart-heavy. Once you have recognized that part of the Shadow that holds you, and once you have released the condition, be prepared to spring back into the Light with a renewed vigour, with a clarity that you didn't have before.

The Heart Chakra develops around the period of seven to nine years of age (although of course this depends on our own experience of life). The experience of opening this Chakra brings with it a sense of self-knowing, which simply put means we begin to make choices for ourselves by ourselves, and for ourselves. These choices occur as decisions about the things in life which appear most significant at the age, for example, food, fluid, succour, clothing, body needs, shelter, rewards and play. Conversely, if we are not given the opportunity to develop 'independence of will', we may become indecisive and vague, finding it difficult to make decisions, and trust.

Discover what is impeding your heart's energy, and consciously bring Alchemy into your life by observing the law of duality reflecting the opposite energy of that you feel. One of the laws of this planet is that "nothing is singular, everything is plural." Although you may feel an intense singular challenge, there are always two existing in duality. For example, if you feel anger or hate, transmute the feeling into joyous freedom and love.

Endeavour to feel the opposite (more favoured state) through the entirety of your body, through the circuit of your cells; it is not accurate to just hold the thought in your head, transform it into feeling through the prism of your heart, and thence through your physical being. And if the 'held' feeling is resistant or stubborn, it will probably have been in your life for some time. So, forgive yourself for experiencing it. Forgive the person or situation that you feel helped to create it. Move into the core of it, shine love and freedom energies like a laser from your heart into the pain, and then move on unencumbered.

Receiving healing from a Practitioner for your Heart Chakra would be a good idea if you find the burden difficult to release or heal yourself. Healing means a movement back to wholeness, and so share with a Counsellor, Healer or a wise Friend. Sound the vowel HA through your heart, thinking/feeling love, and seeing a beautiful green emerald colour washing through and reinstating your heart in unconditional love.

Meditate on freedom and use the Mantra:
" I am free of_____ and my heart is as light as a feather."

STRATEGY TWO:
Do you feel your heart is alight with life?

If you feel your heart is alight with life, qualify: is this truth or illusion? Often we forget that love, joy, laughter, compassion and forgiveness increase serotonin, and release endorphins in our body. The conscious pursuit of these feelings in each moment of life brings us to a state of grace-filled ease.

One of the essential principles to consider is that sustained joy is an indication of success ~ that the greatest achievement we can measure in our lives is that constant joy sustains a harmonious life. This is what produces longevity of success, as *happiness is a decision not a condition.*

I want you to re-member that at the core of the universe is a stream of well-being ~ a flow of force which is the infinite field of unfolding possibility. In the *Source* there is no scarcity or loss. All that we create in our lives has been drawn from this Field through thought, all of it.

Thought and time are 100% evenly present wherever we be. There is never anything missing, for thought creates reality, and all we see without is created by thought. Whatever we feel isn't present in our lives is simply eluding our intelligence. The question is: *"what do you feel about it, and what do you wish to choose?"*

As, *consciousness means choice* what do you want to choose: *pain or pleasure?* There is always a choice between the higher or lower.

Feeling is the language of the soul, and so when our hearts are alight with their higher vibrations, we must give thanks to the Universe with our gratitude. When you feel elevated and alight within your heart immediately begin a rampage of appreciation. This always increases the flow of force, and expands the aura.

Meditate on light-filled success, and use the Mantra:
"I thank the universe with all my heart at the very centre
of my being, for the exquisite joy that I have created.

STRATEGY THREE:
How often do you act compassionately to yourself?

Is compassion, as a living reality, caressing each moment of your existence?

If not, make a list of the times throughout the day when you have actually forgiven yourself for inaccurate doing. After all, if you were inaccurate or inappropriate (let's say callous in behaviour to someone), the action is a product of fear ~ a choice of the lowest vibration of you, not your highest!

Firstly, feel love and mercy radiating from your heart. When you can forgive yourself, when you feel forgiveness sitting in the throne of your heart, you may choose again, and this time more accurately. For when we love ourselves and live mercifully, grace fills our hearts, minds and beings. This leads to unconditional love, when we experience empathy and compassion as supreme visitations of God.

Sometimes we find it easier to forgive others before ourselves, and so this needs readjustment and fairness of value to re-gain balance. Therefore, open yourself to the receiving and giving of the universe to keep your heart healthy. Engage in 'reward-spinning' activities, but not those that are gratuitous. Rather, create activities that are filled with the love and joy of satisfaction and accomplishment. And so, parent the inner child, and give thanks in the form of truly honouring yourself when a successful task is completed.

Observe the life of remarkable master teachers such as Babaji, Jeshua or Buddha; or saints like Mother Teresa, Sri Yukeswar and Yogananda. They gave their lives in the service of love, and through the practice of compassion their acts of generosity were thunderous.

Meditate on compassion and use the Mantra:
"I forgive any of my inaccurate doings and allow my heart to be filled full with forgiveness and mercy!"

STRATEGY FOUR:
How often do you act compassionately to others?

As we review our world we see a paradise of exquisite natural beauty, the Blue Planet. We see drama and calm, we see the awesome height of Mountains and the perplexing depth of Oceans. We see an extraordinary diversity of life, and behaviours, and yet how often do we make a gesture of love to Mother Earth, to the Gaia?

Thought and Feeling are living forces within the Universe. As our planet is microcosmically part of this living symphony, we must cherish the Gaia, feeling compassion for her through simple acts of veneration. From the very depth of our hearts let us become this, and actively live in rapport with her. For, we are fully aware she is ailing, and just as we would care for our own dear Mothers, let us open our hearts and love her into healing. We must reach deep into our hearts and thank her for her continuous and undivided support of our lives ~ through the gravity of her stability, the profundity of her circadian rhythms, the cycle of her seasons, for the fruit and richness of her bio-diversity, reminding us continuously of the trillions of cells in our own bodies:

The Human Cell Of Creation

"When you were first conceived, you were just a double strand fertilized ovum. The ovum then divided fifty times. In only fifty replications, you had become a hundred trillion cells - this is more than all the stars in the Milky Way Galaxy.

Each of these cells is estimated to perform every second about six trillion tasks, and every cell instantly knows what every other cell is doing.

How does a human body think thoughts, play a piano, kill germs, remove toxins, and make a baby all at the same time? Whilst a human body is doing all this, it tracks the movement of the stars and planets, because your biological rhythms are actually the symphony of the Cosmos.

*There's an inner intelligence in your body, and that inner intelligence is **Consciousness**. It is the ultimate in supreme genius, which mirrors the wisdom of the **Universe**."*
- DEEPAK CHOPRA

I suggest living each day with a ritual practice called *Seven Steps To Heaven*. The sixth step of which is to consciously offer a compassionate gift once a day to someone - perhaps this would simply be a smile, a gesture, a kind word, a donation - particularly to those who suffer or those who appear disadvantaged, disempowered or disenfranchised.

The Seven Steps To Heaven

1 Meditate and earth yourself once a day.
2 Speak from your heart - your signature note
   - the song of your soul.
3 Listen to your soul, your higher self.
4 Seek Joy as your first priority.
5 Be a guardian of thought as a living energy.
6 Complete a compassionate deed once each day.
7 Fill your moments with thoughts of grace, and pray for
   peace in your human brothers' and sisters' lives

Fold compassion into your heart for those who are significant to you, particularly those who have done poorly by you. Love both those who are alive, and those who have passed through the veil into infinity.

Meditate on the notion of Namaste ('the divinity within me honors the divinity in you') and use this Mantra:
"I pray for my planetary home, for my fellow brothers and sisters, that I may fill their lives with the light of love from my heart."

STRATEGY FIVE:
Have you consciously eliminated anger from your life?

One of the most coruscating energies that we feel is that of anger. This emotion depletes our life force and creates huge disturbance. And so look into your life, and see the possibility of anger, frustration or irritation lurking in the shadows like a phantom, discontentedly prowling around, until it eventually springs out surprising everyone, including ourselves. Indeed, as we move through the landscape of our lives ~ through city or country, through air or by land, even as we feel joy uplifting our spirits as when we gaze into a source of beauty ~ we may harbour anger somewhere in our bodies. Why?

Mostly because when we were children, we were not given permission to fully feel, express and purge anger. And so ask yourself: when you were young, were you allowed to truly feel anger and to let it burn through you and evaporate into peace? Often this is not so: take for example the occasion when Mother or Father's anger is given precedence over everybody else in the family.

I once heard His Holiness the Dalai Lama say: *"Out with anger, in with love!"* Viewing anger thus gives an indication of what a source of vital energy it can be.

We all experience anger, and yet as children this energy is often so vast and fire-filled that it frightens our caretakers. Consequently, it is seen as inappropriate and we are told to "put it away!" Not knowing where to put it, we stash it away in the fulcrum of our body, until a time comes when it leaks out with every other piece of anger we have felt, or moves inwardly and making us repressed, depressed or ill. These feeling states ravish our bodies and grossly affect our heart and liver - both organs either oxygenate or purify our blood, the flowing force of our love.

When anger is stored away in the unconscious, it ferments and turns into rage, and rage creates war!

If you feel that anger is a choice in your life, I would suggest you ask yourself: what has ever been achieved by using it?

The story of Jesus (John 2:13) in the New Testament turning out the money changers and cattle merchants from the Temple, gives us a clear understanding that when we protest with anger about gross social behaviour, we could be seen to be using anger in a righteous way ~ it is not recorded that Jesus the Master hit or distressed anyone's heart, but rather protested against the inappropriate behaviour and action, which defiled the Temple of his Father's house.

Therefore, be present to your anger and meaningfully express the force when it arises. For example, I've found that beating a cushion helps release the moral outrage I experience in the face of injustice or pain. Or write it out, speak it out, sing it out, love it out, dance it out, paint it out, shout it out ~ for heaven's sake express it in a creatively managed way, rather than spitting it out in someone's face.

Once, I faced the rage of a mugger who pressed his angry face into mine, and held the blade of a knife at my throat. This all took place one lonely night on the London Underground. In my terror I saw my life's power ebbing, and in this state realized I had to find courage somewhere in my heart to love and forgive this man's action. I dug deep into my heart, plumbing its depths before crying from my heart, "I'm sorry, I'm so sorry!" whilst I held his gaze in mine.

The knife dropped and he moved away, and in that moment I realized that this man's anger had never been honoured. His anger had never been accepted by those he loved. Whatever lay at the core of this man's fear and pain, in that moment suddenly evaporated, and I could actually see the energy, like a phantom, leaving him!

Meditate on the release of anger from your own 'Shadow' and use the Mantra:
"I release all my anger or_____ [negative emotional energy] to the Cosmos from whence it came, as I am a child of the universe, and want to live in joy and freedom, as it is intended."

STRATEGY SIX:
Are appreciation and gratitude keys to your living?

Many of us are waking up to the fact that we lack intelligence about our body, and how feeling gratitude for the substance of our physical life is paramount at this time of unprecedented change. For, we must realize that the only way we can truly evolve is by appreciating and loving our bodies, by feeding them with healthy food (favouring fresh vegetables rather than meat), and drinking healthy water – for through the grace of Mother Earth's tears we soften our bodies, as they are 90 per cent fluid, and just as our own Mother fed us with the fluid nectar of life-enhancing milk, so we must nourish life with H_2O. (Read the sacred work of Masaru Emoto in his book *Messages from Water.*)

Furthermore, when our bodies reveal themselves to be sick, we must define why our consciousness led us to illness, and develop instead a healthy rationale by communicating with our cells in a mutual symphony of positive co-creation. Just as we see resourceful collective action prevent severe environmental degradation, toxic poisoning and climate imbalance.

Further still, as we manage the health of our own body we need to find our voice for the ecological and sustainable growth of our planet. Look to Al Gore, who champions this with such truth. As a Nobel Laureate he said: *"There is sometimes a shift in consciousness that moves quickly and suddenly to recognize a new pattern... That's what we're on the cusp of now."*

As we meaningfully move forward through a time of reckoning and new beginnings, we need to release the imbalance of our doing and being - this paranoia created by left brain rationality, believing in the illusion of its own controlling, creates a non-present haze in which we rush our heads from one meeting to another. In moving so fast, we forget our body and un-remember the sublime beauty of heart rending thanks, of appreciation, of gratitude for life ~ of simply seeing how the gift of time is numbered for us, and that to live life in a present fashion is to live life in the moment of NOW.

> **Meditate on all the gifts your life is filled with: your breath, your loved ones, your friends, the beauty of your home, and the passion of your work. Use the Mantra:**
> "I give thanks for the miracle of appreciation and gift of gratitude in my life!"

Creating a list of the things you are grateful for each day brings creative manifestation to the forefront of consciousness. Clear thought functions as an electrical charge, sending the desired creation into the Universe. Then, the feeling associated with the attainment of the dream brings a magnetic charge, through the universal law of attraction. Whatever we wish to create can be found because it already exists somewhere in the Universe.

STRATEGY SEVEN:
Do you make life choices with your heart?

If you are unable to make clear choices from your heart, if you find it difficult to 'dowse with your heart', making decisions filled with joy and hope, the possibility exists that your heart is masked by unhappiness or despair. If this is the case, firstly ask specific questions of yourself for why this is so, and secondly ask your dear ones what their perception is of your ability to decide. Do negative feelings rather than positive states fill you, or does your negativity appear to be the expression of what you see in the environment around you?

The people that come into our lives indicate how positive or negative our inner resources are. For example, this may manifest in the form of a relationship that needs to finish, and yet hasn't terminated because of the fear of loss.

The miracle of life on Planet Earth is that *consciousness means choice,* and in this unfolding there are always two possible instruments that make choice happen. The question is: Do you wish to choose pain or pleasure? Do you wish to create love or hate? In this gift we see the creativity of life reaching into our future through new paradigms. This shift in consciousness means we move from the habit of giving our power away, to becoming the Master/Mistress of our own destiny. So, the key to our future will be the notion of conscious co-creation, not unconscious mis-creation. Please look to the purity of the Masters, for Mastery is the new tool: emulate the Master teachers and their energy will become yours.

Take your heart into the choice of your future creation, no matter how small the choice, no matter how apparently trivial. See the choice of your heart as a new modus, a new job. For example, take your 'heart choice' to the market for buying the vegetables and fruit, or for the many other decisions you make - this in essence is what I mean by 'heart dowsing'.

When you meet someone new, when you receive a perception in regard of something you have done, always 'dowse with your heart'. Take the decision to your Heart, observe that every choice you make is a fresh response to a heartfelt want, and not just a reaction to that you have always unconsciously made.

Too often we are negatively affected by the perception of others. Therefore, each time someone offers an idea of your conduct, perceive first if it is a projection. Remember, it is only a perception and isn't necessarily accurate. Here I refer to the observation that people often try to control the situation they find themselves in by employing a host of generalities, or perceptions, that can be used like weapons to merely gain supremacy over an individual or a situation. These are commonly known as 'control dramas', and may be observed as behavioural mechanisms that evoke certain states in us. Take, for example, the Perfectionist and the Aloof, or the Bully and the Poor Me.

Many of us unconsciously develop control dramas as strategies to control other people, and therefore draw from their energy field the nourishing force we cannot create for ourselves. The Perfectionist or Interrogator controls behaviour by never allowing anyone to express their creativity, for you have to do it their way. The Aloof attempts responding to the Interrogator, but never succeeds, and therefore develops the unconscious behaviour of aloofness - refusing to respond to anyone. For example, check out the behaviour of the stereotypical adolescent.

Likewise, the Bully or Intimidator is the angry, threatening person, who uses aggression to receive energy. If we accept punishment from the Bully, we become feeble as a Poor Me: meaning someone who is conditioned to constantly feel unwell or abandoned.

It's simple. If you are not feeling good, if your energy is unclear and makes you feel weak or despairing, you are not in connection with the Source. There is no point in fretting over such conditions, and so release the person, cure the pain immediately from your consciousness. Sai Baba once said: *"What's the point of worrying when you can pray!"*

Meditate on your hierarchy of values and use the Mantra:
"I love the opportunity my life gives me to be as clear as spring water by 'heart dowsing' my every choice!"

(Dowsing, sometimes called 'divining' refers to the practice of detecting hidden water or Ley Lines, without the use of scientific apparatus. Instead, Dowsing Rods are used)

STRATEGY EIGHT:
Are you sentimental in the use of your heart?

The great poet and author James Joyce wrote: *"Sentimentality is unearned emotion."* Often we engage in emotional states that are generalized and awash with mawkishness. These are states of behaviour that lack clarity because we are consumed by 'attachment' to things that give us the illusion of being secure, whereas in reality we merely use the association to bolster our uncertain sense of self.

The true definition of the word Secure is Self-Cure, and not the giving away of personal power by attachments that appear to measure security. These forms are status, income, costly clothes or adornments, extravagant mortgages or fast cars.

When we are touched by something, we must manage the force of our hearts with true discernment, and not just react to the condition, simply because we are in truth fearful of losing it.

> *It is important to know that you can disappoint another person to be true to yourself. It is important to know that you can bear the accusation of betrayal and not betray your own soul. It is important to know that you can be seen to be lacking in faith, but trustworthy to the cause of your own truth.*
> FROM 'THE INVITATION,' BY ORIAH MOUNTAIN DREAMER

I do not wish to give the impression that by this I'm suggesting a rigid capturing of feeling, but rather that emotion is 'energy in motion', and feeling takes us to the very core of our state; for feeling is the language of the soul. Therefore, if we are experiencing higher states such as Love & Joy, we are in clear reflection of Source Energy, and when we feel grosser energies such as Despair & Unworthiness, we are merely holding ourselves in Ego and denying the existence of Spirit!

Once we have the ability to qualify and discern feeling energies, we develop emotional intelligence about the essence of 'feeling' from the point of view of it being a physical sensation:

> *"to experience a state of being which can be loosely, profanely or divinely writ."*
> - WILLIAM SHAKESPEARE

In the prologue to this book I write:

> *"The heart is not a sentimental organ, it is forthright, brave and substantial. It supports and nourishes all systems of the body during a life-long commitment to excellence. Moreover, the intelligence of the heart has within it a beat, a power, that signals the next level of development within the survival of our species."*

When our hearts experience the joy and awe that lead to soul-worship, we start an altogether different way of being. If we can truly acknowledge that our souls are ripened by our feelings, we begin a faith-filled journey of great mystery, an awakened life. This calls us to a time that is specifically measured by intelligent action articulated through the ritual I encourage of *Silence, Solitude and Stillness.*

Silence takes us to the deepest place within ourselves, to the intensity, intimacy and immensity of our souls. For these characteristics are the hall-marks of the 'mystical experience' and take us to the very crucible of the heart. There we encounter the extreme beauty of a natural landscape, the exquisite tenderness of humanity, the soaring spirit of the artist, the teacher who incubates imagination, the humility of the child's cry.

All of these move us from lush sentimentality into the awesome nature of the maturing heart. Then the mind connected to the heart becomes enlightened and produces wisdom. Please let awe and not sentimentality be the beginning of your wisdom.

Meditate on the clear expression of heartfelt feeling in your life and use the Mantra:
"I yield to the wisdom of my heart, as a crucible for the Divine to instruct me in the expression of qualitative feeling."

STRATEGY NINE:
Do you love to receive and give in your life?

Life in the fast lane doesn't always allow us to measure the quality of our receiving, in relation to the quantity of our giving. Indeed, the 'monkey chatter' of 'doing' often leads us to an awareness of output which is unfairly reckoned against the nature of our input.

As awareness of this imbalance is a central construct of my work, I've written at length about 'doing and being' in other areas of this book. So lett's simply observe how interesting it is to note how the actions of doing and being are so closely aligned to the very nature of giving and receiving, and so may be weighed in similar fashion.

The way that folk open or close their hearts to love, to the possibility of giving, tells us so much about them as people. Are their hearts open to the flower of all graces, that of generosity? When giving simply flows as an act of love wanting nothing in return, the grace of heaven infuses all with ease. Conversely, how many people have you met who only give to receive, and how many people do you know who look truly embarrassed when receiving, so much so that they literally give up giving? It's a conundrum.

Whatever your normal process may be about the action of giving and the response of receiving: examine it, discuss it with friends and loved ones, try to formulate a higher choice as you lift awareness into the clarity of the great light. You will possibly find that the ebb and flow of your own generosity, to other people as well as to self, is so taken for granted that there are issues lurking between its folds.

Qualify this force within your life's journey, and see how the power of giving and receiving compassionately can bring joy into your life. If we can complete a generous act each day for a living being or creature, we take one further step towards heaven. Notice, that when this is a commitment, when nothing is wanted in return, life becomes filled with moments of bliss that passeth all understanding.

Giving and Receiving through the vestibules of the heart portrays what we are being: the fundamental energies of our yang (male) and yin (female) force. This is an archetypal evaluation, and so the next time you are in an intimate moment of life - in the expression of lovemaking for example - observe how you display or utilize these energies.

Meditate on the substance of how you give and receive. Make up your own Mantra, or use:
"I live and love to express my creative force through the fundamental flow of giving and receiving. I ask the Spiritual Masters and Angels to bless me, and to inform me kindly about the moments when I haven't freely loved, so that I may heal and transform."

STRATEGY TEN:
What work do you engage in to alleviate the suffering of others?

This strategy is a confirmation of our quality of contribution to each other's lives. It is a reminder of the absolute inclusivity of life, that all planetary living is contained within the circle of our extraordinary planet and beyond. Just as sacred geometry gives us the circle as a form to echo the Divine Feminine, all force, all quanta, moves forward and yields to the nature of that that has been created.

The Alchemical symbol of the Ouroborus reflects that beginning is an ending, and thus an ending is a beginning ~ the alpha and the omega. The Ouroborus is an ancient symbol representing the creative principle. It is classically depicted as a Serpent chasing and swallowing its own tail, and thereby evolving through an eternal returning. What is implied, is that all forms end and begin.

Our daily thought must be: are we committed to healing ourselves and then to helping others heal, to alleviating the suffering of others? Can we do this by simply observing that pain is a cry for freedom, and that the soul's action is made mute by the very nature of suffering in order to find itself, rather than in judging another's pain? Can we see that healing determines the soul's distress, because its vital force has become obscured by a sense of separation from *Source*?

If suffering means that a soul has been captured by the illusion of the Ego, a soul that functions thus lives in separation from all other souls, and cannot feel its own unique aspect, role or purpose in the delivery of creation.

In contribution to our lives, my role as a Sound Healer through 'The Alchemy Of Voice' facilitates a twelve-part canon of works, the second of which is entitled Initiation. This workshop is concerned with the liberation of a magnificent conviction: that the soul wishes to meet its own unfolding, its pathway of incarnation, by truly acknowledging the rite of initiation as a tool for survival.

Revealed within its teaching is the heartfelt encouragement of the great "I AM Presence." This is a process concerning one of the most profound wisdoms handed down to us by the Masters. For the proclamation of I AM is an inner acceptance of acknowledging that the creative essence of God in the Universe is within us, and that the more we identify with our human self as a reflection of the sacred, the more we relate to our Divine presence made incarnate: so we are one with God.

Jesus said: *"I am the way the truth and the life, without the way there is no going, without the truth there is no living."* He wished to teach the vital knowledge that all of life is sacred, no one is better or lesser, we are all souls incarnated to optimize our creative energy through love and joy.

PASSAGE OF GRACE: Marianne Williamson wrote the most wonderful song of praise for the I AM Presence, encapsulated in these words:

> *Our deepest fear is not that we are inadequate.*
> *Our deepest fear is that we are powerful beyond measure.*
> *It is our light, not our darkness, that most frightens us.*
> *We ask ourselves who are we to be brilliant,*
> *gorgeous, talented, fabulous?*
> *Actually, who are we not to be?*

You are a child of God.
Your playing small doesn't serve the world.
There is nothing enlightened about shrinking, so that
other people won't feel insecure around you.
We were born to make manifest the glory of God
that is within us.
It's not just in some of us; it's in everyone.
And, as we let our own light shine, we unconsciously
give other people permission to do the same.
As we are liberated from our own fear
our presence automatically liberates others!

By living these words, we contribute to the alleviation of suffering in our brothers and sisters. By moving to these words we activate our God presence, and so heal self from separation. We see that an awareness of the Ego with regard to the *Source* is incompatible. By speaking and affirming these words, we strike the note of our own creation, a story that is reaching forth at this time as we exceed our reach through a quantum grasp, and reveal to ourselves the ladder to heaven.

Meditate on the substance of compassion in your life and the lives of your brothers and sisters. Use the Mantra:
"I am alive with the beauty of life in this moment of NOW, and venerate this moment as sacred. Thereby, I am improving the vibration of thought that permeates the consciousness of this most exquisite planet."

STRATEGY ELEVEN:
Are you lovingly healing the 'Heart Stabs' of life?

This strategy refers to those challenging feelings that seemingly conspire against us, and turn all sensation into a bloody emotional battlefield. These are the invectives that stab our hearts, robbing us of our happiness, making us disharmonic and unwell with unhappiness.

Emotions like:
Fear
Anger
Grief
Guilt

Self-blame
Worry
Sadness
Depression
Despair

To transcend these 'Heart Stabs', to effectively heal the wound of remorse, so that you don't continuously re-feel the emotion: take the situation, person, stimuli or scenario fully into your heart, take it fully into the loving secret chamber of your heart. Take everything, take all the detailing and all the strife, and on your knees ask God or the Source to release the negative hurt from you, to heal you forever. Let go to love, and let God in!

By processing in this way you will heal the hurt in your heart and body, you will cease the percolation of energies that keep taking you back to the memory or thought or action. You will cease obsessively regurgitating the process of hurt and the storyline from which it springs. For we all remember the moments in life, such as waking refreshed from a good night's sleep, and then disturbing events from the previous day crash into our consciousness, disturbing the peace of the night's recovery.

Having felt free for a moment, having felt detached from obsessive behaviour, we once again begin to anxiously fret over and over and over the challenge; again and again we disturb and upset ourselves. No solution is ever gained by this. Whereas the power of prayer is documented as a transcendent force, so please reflect on its use, and you will see how I utilize it later in this book.

When we seize the moment, seeing that the apparent crisis is an opportunity for radical change, for a fervent revolution of consciousness, our decisive actions allow us to fully determine what we feel, and cut through to the hurt; instead of being consumed by the re-actions and pain, we respond afresh, launching our emotional GPS system.

Joy raises the vibration of despair, for joy through forgiveness washes the hurt. This way holds powerful purification and in consequence, we heal ourselves, our lives and our relationships, returning back to love, back to the whole holy - for to be spiritual is to be in touch with whole-ness.

All relationships are significant, as they are part of the radiating confluence of our energy. Even those slight personal connections we call acquaintances, all are created by us, all are ways of expressing our divine status, all are opportunities to move away from the lower vibrations and the profane.

With this in mind, bolster your heart healing process by using Alchemy. Discern what lies within the emotion: what is the feeling called, where do you feel it in your body, what colour is it, and to which Chakra is the feeling connected? For all can be alchemically relieved within the vibrational frequency of Planet Earth, as nothing is singular, everything is plural. Therefore, where fear lies so does freedom exist, where grief lurks so does joy behold, not lurking in the shadows but rather existing in a state of illumination.

"Joy and woe are woven fine
A clothing for the soul divine;
Under every grief and pine
Runs a joy with silken twine.

It is right, it should be so;
Man was made for joy and woe
And when this we rightly know
Safely through the world we go."
- *WILLIAM BLAKE*

The feeling states of joy and woe are the two sides of the same coin. They create the nature of emotional paradox. The list of emotional paradoxes reaches off into infinity: guilt/innocence, victim/victor, illusion/truth, depression/expression, despair/hope, impotency/potency, self-loathing/self-loving, worry/faith. Furthermore, there is a belief in Native America that if a snake bites you, the antidote lies but twenty feet away (6 meters). All you have to do is find it!

The wondrous work that has arisen from the laboratory of *Emotional Intelligence*, brought initially to our attention by Daniel Goleman in 1996, and thence the earth shaking *The HeartMath Solution*, published in 2000 by Doc Childre & Howard Martin, also follow through this 'heart cut-through technique' with surprising efficacy.

The human heart has a seismic power both within the life to which it is dedicated, and the life of the planet on which it resides. It is well documented that the human heart generates an electro-magnetic field far stronger than any other organ within the body, the power of which is 5,000 times greater than the human brain.

This literally means that the heart's energy field has been scientifically measured from six to eight feet (2 meters) outside the body and beyond. The potential of this information is outstanding, for if this field of resonance were created by a specific heart choice from the collective population of Mother Earth, the field of energy would measure by miles (km) not feet (mtr).

The heart's magnetic field responds in each moment of our lives to the emotions we create within this field of energy. Each feeling state affects our bodies through the balance or imbalance of hormones, the flow of blood, water and plasma, the rhythm or anti-rhythm of heart energy, cellular degeneration or regeneration, the depression or expression of physical force; by each feeling our hearts responsively communicate with the space or locale in which we are placed.

Therefore, the emotional impact of a life event in turn affects our internal processing and creative output; in effect, the whole of our creative force in the world becomes charged with heart radiation.

When our emotions are positive, there is an increase of biological activity that stimulates our heart energy as well as brain activity. Our energy field responds, and joyous manifestations occur in our lives. This produces mental clarity and increased creativity. Whereas when negative emotions occur, over one thousand bio-chemical changes rapidly stimulate heart-rhythm chaos, adrenalin and cortisol hyper-activity, muscular aches, and the mental confusions that lead to weak performance, unstable productivity and poor relationships.

In September 2001, two geostationary operational environment satellites, in orbit 22,300 miles (35,880 km) over the equator of Planet Earth, detected a huge shift in the Globe's magnetic field that forever altered the way science views the planet. These powerful shifts occurred fifteen minutes after the first plane hit the World Trade Centre on September 11th, and again fifteen minutes before the second plane hit.

Studies conducted by Princeton University in the United States and the non-profit organization HeartMath found that the correlation between the registered shifts in the earth's magnetic field and the events of 9/11 were more than a coincidence. The satellites had registered similar activity during the tragic events of August 31st 1997, when Princess Diana died.

This indicates quite clearly that the emotional intention arising from the heart of the people affects the magnetic field of the globe, and therefore clarifies a brilliantly divine plan ~ if the magnetic fields are stimulated by every feeling that is produced in response to war and peace, economic scarcity or abundance, societal loss or gain, climate tragedy or climate balance - human emotionality is the leading edge frontier for human evolution.

If we can effectively learn the language of the heart, we can alter the earth's magnetic field, and in so doing we alter the power of the effect that 'the field' has upon all planetary life. For the first time in the evolution of the human species we can consciously, advantageously alter all life through the interconnectivity of our planet.

Meditate on the enormity of these findings, these essential declarations of the creative movement on our planet. Tune into the Global Coherence Initiative on-line, and observe the interface between Science and Spirituality arising from the contemporary wisdom culture and use the Mantra:

"I release all of my hurts. I deactivate all of the 'Heart Stabs' I've experienced, and send their force to the greatness of the Source. I work to transmute all ill, and move joyously on the path of wholeness."

STRATEGY TWELVE:
Do you consciously celebrate the 'Heart Tingles' of life?

In a world where 'violence' and 'disagreement' are used as a currency for change, whether this be nation fighting nation, husband fighting wife, or child fighting child ~ statistics show that physical violence occurs within four to six million intimate relationships each year in the United States, and the actual statistics are probably much higher because this form of violence is often unreported.

It is time to actively celebrate the 'Heart Tingles' of life, to seek ways of elevating our consciousness away from the rigours and incarceration of secular thought. We need to release ourselves from these straitjackets and undertake a mode of celebration by creating individual rituals for:

Love
Compassion
Non-judgment
Courage
Patience
Sincerity
Forgiveness
Appreciation
Gratitude

Much of this book encourages the active stimulation of these feelings, that through conscious daily acts of 'heart dowsing' and 'heartfelt tingling' we may recover the language of the heart, which we once lived. This is a path to happiness, a way of developing more harmonious relationships, a modus by which we individually become much healthier, a way of regulating our emotions that become the next frontier of human evolution.

Try an experiment: take each heart tingle one day at a time into your daily life. Literally, for nine days (the ancient number of completion) ritualize the observation of each degree. As thought creates reality, as feeling manifests actuality, you will experience a huge shift in your consciousness where heart energy pulsates with renewed vigour, and feeling good will utterly change the creative expression of your life, and of those around you.

These quality feelings will bring such happiness to your journey, and as happiness brings with it divine action in the world of form, it helps to sustain our souls and our unique effectiveness. Each heart tingle is a magnificent seed whereby you may step into co-creation with God, and live the originality of each step, thus illuminating your pathway.

> *"The spiritual path is a high energy phenomenon in a very tired world. It's outside the limits of the secular box that dominates our social dialogue. Mystical thought is trivialized, diminished, even labelled inane by our cultural gatekeepers, but spiritual concepts are breaking into the vernacular despite materialistic resistance. Those who obstruct the spiritual conversation are standing in the way of an urgently needed unfoldment."*
> *- MARIANNE WILLIAMSON FROM HER INSPIRATIONAL AND COURAGEOUS BOOK, ILLUMINATA.*

Meditate on the power of these heart tingles and by fulfilling the suggestion... Life Will Pulsate With Excitement, as You Use The Mantra:
"I love to activate the 'heart tingles' of life, and will become one of their ardent lovers, facilitating each one in each moment of my living."

†he Hear† Voice

*The holiest of all places on Earth is where an ancient
hatred has become a present love.*
- HH THE DALAI LAMA

To be sound in heart and mind is an ancient precept, and one of life's creative imperatives. To find sound foundation, to build sound judgement in a time when standards of living, social mores and established structures are powerfully and dramatically changing, means that we may evolve and mature as secure and discerning people.

Truth to tell, new life always takes form when we are chastened and humbled by ordeal. When we are sorely challenged and fall to our knees, supplication carves out who we truly are; cleansed and unadorned by the ego, we begin afresh, wiser for the counsel, if somewhat scarred.

The Art Of Sounding

In Europe during the sixteenth century, the art of 'sounding' was known as an instrument for plumbing the depths of the human body, as well as a means by which the depth of water could be discerned. In each case, sounding was used to discern that which appears unknown, and wishes to become knowable.

When we reach out to gain knowledge, we seek truth. For what are we without the authentic, who are we without the relative value, where are we without a point of reckoning and whom shall we be without the mystery of faith? Being taken to the altar of mystery means that we dedicate ourselves to knowing the unknowable.

Once we are sound in mind and body and we wish to express our content, reach out to communicate essence from the very centre of our observation. Thus, we open to veracity, and speak with plumbed truth, using a power of resonance from the deep waters of our interior being. It is then that our listeners empathetically hear, and they become magnetically drawn to be witness to the act.

But this only happens when we are alive to our bodies as temples of feeling and sensing. This happens when we live in the power of the present withholding nothing, expressing ourselves as being sound in heart and mind. For, to forge deep, satisfying and authentic relationships, to live in the essence of what we may become, it is essential that we communicate truthfully and without illusion. If truth is absent, we encounter confusion, which inevitably scatters our ability to create fresh, responsible, harmonious and newly awakened relationships. As the heart is the organ of truth, if truth is absent from our living, our hearts diminish in their stature.

We must heed the call of this time to expand the greatness of our hearts, for this is a time when the desire to grow through the peak awareness of adversity is paramount. We must develop sound systems of personal management, through techniques mitigated by emotional intelligence. We must open our hearts, and live with love, empathy, mercy, compassion and grace.

For as we interpret these signs and sound the very signature note of our beings, our hearts enchant their yearning into existence. This is so when we hear the very silence of nature, when we are moved by the holy wind, and when we are humbled by our own magnificence as when life is revealed by a wise oracle.

Similarly, this is a time of prophecy, given by the indigenous people of our world, a time for our hearts to be opened and be made wise by experience, understanding and knowledge. For they as wisdom-keepers know that our hearts have a secret chamber from which the lives of our souls can be spoken.

From the most ancient of calls, from deep within us, from the fortitude of our consciousness wishing to reveal itself as an organ of grace, we hear a note that doesn't just spring from intellectual endeavour alone. This note tells the full story of who we truly are, as spiritual beings on a human journey, living in a vastly connective network of intelligence, and potential grace. For within our signature note, within our heart's chamber lies the blueprint of our psyche, which is the very song of our soul.

If we hear the human voice as a means for revelation, a conduit by which to proclaim our heart's knowing, an organ through which we may harmonize the totality of our being, do all listen and fully hear the statement of its power? We hear this when Barack Obama speaks, for we all listen.

Through this intelligence, through this consciousness, we move from negative disenchantment into knowing what is enchanting about our lives. For please know that within your signature note, resonating from your heart is the blueprint of your humanity and the seat of your soul; this is your Genesis.

And so here is a special Meditation that will take you to plumbing the depths of your soul, taking you to your soul's song, your signature note. This will take you into the secret chamber of your heart, where your soul rings clearly forth as an anointed bell, as a clarion call fully celebrating life.

The Heart's Note ~ Meditation

- Make sure you are within your own Sacred Space for this unique creation, the sounding of your Heart's note. Check that you won't be disturbed by switching on 'voicemail'.
- Soften the light within the space, burn a candle (a symbol of the greater Light that lightens all consciousness), burn incense to purify your intention, place a sacred icon on your Altar: a picture of one of the Great Masters, such as Jesus or Buddha, Mary or Quan Yin.
- You may even have a bell to ring gently, clearing the air and reminding you of purity, calling you to the gentleness of prayer as a mode of speaking to God.
- Make sure that your body is in a position where you can sit with your spine aligned, your hands placed comfortably, with the tip of thumb and forefinger lightly touching. Feel that there is gravity in your body, that your feet are touching the floor when sitting in a chair, or that the base of your spine is in contact with the floor if you are sitting cross-legged. Remove your shoes.

BE STILL for a moment and tune into the *Silence* around you. Within silence there is a space where the infinity of soul is palpable.

- Imagine a laser beam of light moving through your spine.
- See the colour of it moving into Mother Earth.
- See the colour of it moving up and off into Father Heaven.
- Then, breathe out all the air in your body through your lips.
- Wait, and in a moment, feel the need to breathe.
- Then, breathe in Life Force through your nostrils.
- See this Force as a colour moving through your spine.
- Breathe wide and deep with this colour of Chi.
- Then breathe out all the energy 'held' within.

We will do this 7 times and then Sound the Divine Elements...

Earth   *Haw*   Feel the resonance in your pelvis area

Water	*Hoo*	Feel the resonance in your solar plexus
Air	*How*	Feel the resonance in your throat centre
Fire	*Hee*	Feel the resonance in your head
	Haa	Feel the resonance in your heart centre

Haa & Hum, Hum, Hum, Hum in your heart…

- Feel the four currents of the sonic shower through the whole of your spine, through the entirety of your being.
- This harmonic shower will resonate through your whole physical geometry, and you may want to chant a mantra as a gift to the Divine, such as OM.

When you are completely relaxed, listen to a distant sound…

- Feel the rhythm of your breath moving deeply in your being, representing the inspiration of the dynamic force in your life and the Universe.
- Feel how the rest of your body and mind are completely still.
- Here you will feel yourself standing like a mountain and flowing like a river.
- Connect with each sense and thus feel truly Present with the Now ~ the vastness of the Space you feel within and without as you soak in Soul. You will feel the Anima Mundi, the universal current of the Love Light Circuitry, the Morphogenetic Field. The Source is a space of utter well being that is an infinitely unfolding possibility of Divine Creation.
- Just soak in this feeling for as long as you can. Remember this, for this is a high calling.
- Process the images, visions or counsel that are provided for you in these sacred moments. Receive teaching from your Guides or the Angels.
- Feel sheathed or protected by your energy field, filled with the purity and presence of your soul's light, and reconnected with the harmony of unity consciousness.
- You have just successfully moved into your Heart using your Signature Note as a talisman, as a sonic key opening the sensation of absolute truth….this is the Secret Chamber of your heart.
- You may feel filled with divine inspiration, touched with a sacred elixir, in the Nowness Of Now, or in possession of an insight about

your life or your loved ones, simply aware of refined 'well being' soaking through the whole of your consciousness.

- Many things take place within the temple of your body whilst engaging in this practise: the ability to bring about heart-brain coherence, the chemical and physical resonance of harmony, the sacred observation of your signature note, the emotional gathering of empathy, the mental clarification of concepts, the spiritual ascendency of your Pranic Being, and a sense of your own personal sovereignty ~ the great I AM PRESENCE.

- All this and more will occur as you move into a symphony of alignment with all your brothers and sisters, and the expanse of the whole natural world or Cosmos. This is a Global Coherence strategy of unquestionable importance.

The Secret Chamber

The secret chamber of your heart is like a Crystal Cave where a great Magician resides. In the silence, the Magician will gift you with a connection to the most precious of cosmic forces, the portal presence of universal co-creativity.

The energy centre of your Heart Chakra (a spinning wheel of fire) will allow you to partake of a quintessential remembering, an utter sense of whom you truly are as a quanta of light: human and yet suffused with the divine, and therefore of what is most precious.

The Heart Chakra

We will return to the secret chamber of the heart, its physical and metaphysical vision, legacy and portent, in a later chapter. In the meantime the prophecy offered about this secret chamber is also in alignment with the Hindu/Buddhist Chakra practice.

The ancient Sanskrit name for the heart chakra is Anahata meaning "the sound that is made without two things striking: the un-struck or unhurt note."

I have found that one remarkable aspect of life is how suddenly we may stumble upon a finding which reveals an innate aspect of our being-ness — a some-thing that has hitherto remained submerged in the deeper recesses of our consciousness, secreted beyond our ken, hidden somewhere in the fractals of light known as space-time. Seemingly, unwittingly, and yet truly directed by our own spiritual GPS (the law of attraction), we discover a shaft of light that has thus far not shown itself.

The testament of our heart is, that once open, the Anahata compels us to stop harm and hurt being caused, for opening the heart means that one is automatically hardwired, one is empathetically programmed for love and peace:

"No man with a peace filled heart
can see the blood of violence written on the sky."
- CHIEF BLACKFOOT 1860

More About The Heart's Secret

The secret chamber of the heart, used for dreaming by the Planet's indigenous people, teaches us that all life is sacred, and that destruction is in diametric opposition to creation. Therefore, war must cease. At the very least we must refrain from causing harm to all living things.

When people are not held by the spectre-power of harm, they release themselves from fear-based defensive behaviour. They become free in essence to be what they truly are. Free to create abundantly, free to contribute something rich and profound to the lives of others and the life of the planet. Free to fall asleep at night knowing that our talents, our love, our lives were used to serve others.

For our most basic virtue is to love, and we are most free, we are most powerful, our Creator's presence is most apparent on earth, when we are jubilant with this love. Love gives energy and direction. It is spiritual fuel.

Love Will Perpetuate

This quality of freedom requires a level of sophistication that supersedes domination and aggression. This freedom introduces the virtues of cooperation and kindness. Moreover, each time we experience life through these qualities, we experience a paradise where the whole of nature whispers that something magnificent is happening, and as this intention is carried by the wind, somewhere someone breathes deeply, and life is restored.

This intention and volition for peace is a powerful possibility in our lives. In February 2003, ten million citizens all over the world marched in peaceful protest for the cessation of war, relatively at the same time and on the same day, even though many lived in countries not directly affected by the chaos of what was impending. The immanent war was created by the then-President of the United States George Bush in order to subdue terrorism borne out by the country of Iraq. This war encouraged young Iraqi men and women to embark on suicide missions and blow themselves to pieces.

These facts horrify. For the only way to cease such senseless acts of terrorism is to create a world where the existence of war is simply unimaginable. The conviction of our love, rather than the conviction of our hatred, allows us to heal, and in opening the chamber of the heart we are led to a peace that brings manna from heaven.

Like manna directly from heaven, we may feel that within our heart chakra is a note which amplifies the divine sound of our being, and when our voice sounds this note, our physical, emotional, mental and spiritual energies have the possibility to vibrate a powerful cry. Remember the story of Joshua and his men in the Old Testament? They marched around the city of Jericho, they gave a great shout, and the walls of Jericho came tumbling down.

Finding Your Soul's Sound

If you find the fundamental note of something, you can also find a way of creating or destroying that thing. Remember the story of the singer making a crystal glass ring with her note. When the singer's ability moved the note past the harmonic balance of the glass, the glass smashed.

We are possibly doing this every day of our lives, and the majority of people are completely unaware of the fact that this is what they are doing. Conversely, if we dwell in harmony manifesting sound from 'centred' lives, we begin to stand on the shoulders of giants. We live the integrity and joy that is our birthright.

The ancients called this *Persona* meaning "*through sound.*" Each time we create our signature note, our note of harmony, our bodies balance and our cells evolve more healthily. Literally, we can feel this, as our bodies vibrate in tune with the symphony of the Galaxy. In our cellular song, our biological rhythms harmonize with the whole orchestra of the Cosmos as we sound our heart's note.

For you see, the hundred trillion cells within your being are a microcosm of the Cosmos, and reflect the macrocosm with its many stars shining throughout the Milky Way. What is more is that your note has an echo, which has resounded throughout the Cosmos since the moment of your birth, your first roar of this life, and its vibration is recorded in the great esoteric hall of records known as the Akashic.

As you mature through your living, the signature note of your creation encourages you into an expression of the very author-ship of you, for true authority means we reclaim the connection with our past, a past where the movement of modern science de-sacralised nature, severing our mind's connection from our bodies, splitting thought from feeling, and psyche from soma. So your signature note's 'awakening' becomes an even greater truth; it heralds a fully embodied natural state, vibrating with all of life.

Our Sovereignty Matters

This act returns us to our personal sovereignty. For as we govern our free will, we become initiated into governing ourselves, and to be open to our social responsibility. So we may live triumphant within the temple of our physical flesh, at core of which sits our heart-throne, with the potential to resonate throughout the kingdom of our lives. This is a mythic or archetypal reckoning, when the supreme realm of the soul opens us to our personal hierarchy, and so we live inspirationally.

The clarion call of God's will always directs us by inspirational means, and so we discover our true calling. This is not to just 'do' whatever that thing is that one needs to do, but more importantly to 'be' the love and creativity that lies at the very core of one's spirit, and so to feel real pleasure derived from God's will.

However, firstly we often choose to wake through desperation, for crisis forces us to examine and reflect upon our very core. Here we find forgotten aspects of ourselves, hidden in the shadow of the inner wounded child crying out for healing. Through counselling, through healing, through time, and lots of loving, we bring balance back to our masculine (doing) and feminine (being), and so we begin to exist more easily in relationship with ourselves.

We may be humbled and chastened by ordeal, we may be bloody and bruised but not defeated, for we have valiantly broken out of the confines of cultural conformity, and have shuffled off the tribe whose 'shadow warfare' of obligation, duty, should and ought, have clung to us through conditions, like shackles that once held us. Finally, we are free to breathe and sound the force of our own liberation, and to set forth on a path of unconditional love.

Of course, before we can be liberated no one escapes the pain of feeling hurt anywhere along the journey. Loss and disappointment, betrayal and wounding, trauma and abandonment come to all of us and leave their scars on our hearts and bodies. If we fortress our hearts in consequence, we live a sense of terrible isolation.

A fortress of personal and social contempt brings us to war against ourselves, or those dear ones that may try to reach out to us; whereas, the process this writing offers is one that struggles to change old belief systems, and to find out solutions that teach us new paradigms and behaviours, that stealthily but compassionately transform blame and accusation into insight and resolution.

When we face this degree of resolution in ourselves, our task is then to face our societal shadow through the complexities of domination, hatred, greed and violence. For these are controls that spring like vipers from the nest of fear. Our innate values, our social fabrics, our economic status, all must be revolutionized, all must change, if we are to see our cognitive faculties in alignment with emotional intelligence, if we are to see our nurturing skills balanced with our sense of accomplishment.

Then and only then will our received knowledge be equalled by our intuitive wisdom. Then we will be collectively victorious, and our world cultures will change - just as we have acquired a unique personal freedom, just as we have vast reserves of extraordinary knowledge, just as we find ourselves at a unique point of evolution through our systems of communication technology. For this is the first time in human history that we have the extent and nature of informed thought literally at our fingertips through information technology, so too, do we have the shadow side of our personal and societal power creating tyranny and desecration.

The environmental holocaust, the proliferation of nuclear or biological weapons, the fixation with fossil fuels, religious fundamentalism, the lack of media coherence, the wasted intelligence relating to our addiction to science and controlled reasoning – all of these are mechanisms that dramatically move us away from our essential core.

How Old Are Your Emotions?

Our emotions reach back a hundred million years, whilst our cognitions are merely a few hundred thousand years old. So there is a sense of cosmic youthfulness about our beings, wishing to break through adolescence and find a personality, a new note and a new power. Just as we mature in life, we release the complex and compound difficulties, and aspire to our soul's growth.

When there is a release of force from old ways, when expression is a gentle hum of peace, there is expressed from us a unique vibration beheld by all, a harmony that brings with it a sense of awe, a visitation of the celestial, a feeling of deep stillness.

When the constructs of the fortress have been fully dismantled, when the wounds are healed, then there is more space. The fortress of the ego instead becomes the realm of the soul where we are free to breathe, to relax, to embody the light.

The sounding of our note is an act of love, an act of devotion, and an act of grace. If we live this, our love suffuses each of our daily thoughts and actions, and to be this self-sustaining, we need to open ourselves to the devotional pathway.

The Temple Of Love

Service to a higher purpose means we tap into paradigms that support us through sacred gifts as ladders to God. A daily spiritual practice initiated in our own sacred space enriches connection with our heart, our community, our planet, our galaxy, our cosmos, our love, and ultimately with our God.

If in each day we can make our lives a little better than we began them, if we can open our arms to the miracle of creation, and make life more beautiful than we found it, then we truly give of our love. Each time we give an act of love we inspire someone else to do the same, and so the Temple of Paradise is created here on Earth. If we let what we love to resonate loudly in the centre of our lives, if we allow it to occupy every inch, every gram, and every breath, we achieve something as a gift to immortality.

The question is how do we constructively achieve this, when so much of life is filled with ephemera? How can we create lives of purpose in a world that seems preoccupied with the drama of the latest news? If we cast an eye over sound practices associated with religious or spiritual welfare, there is always hope. If we are to be made certain of whom we are, we must become the portal keepers of discipline.

The Twelve Grace Code

Nine hundred years ago the Knights Templar gave their lives in protective service to devoted Christians, when on pilgrimage to Jerusalem. They acted as Guardians for the faithful as they touched the lodestone and birthplace of their belief.

The Temple Knights are also known as the mythical Guardians of the Holy Grail, and the Arc of the Covenant. Legends suggest they lived an honour code, which through discerning meditation and disciplined prayer led to the victory of enlightenment. The code consisted of twelve graces, the seed elements from which mighty miracles may grow, and each grace indicates a major area of life from which the heart may be kindled, nourished, loved and enchanted into its own burgeoning.

When we seek expression of our spiritual warrior-ship we convene our heart as part of a cellular whole, we see our role in the heart of the world as an act of service, holding the precious jewels of liberty, rightness and honesty as powerful keys to the noble mind.

The Honour Code consists of Twelve Graces:

LOVE
TRUTH
JOY
PIETY
HUMILITY
FAITH
MERCY
WISDOM
LOYALTY
COURAGE
JUSTICE
VICTORY

LOVE

Love is what we are created from and born with. The opposite of love is what we learn here on Earth. Love, like a lotus, opens our hearts when we truly appreciate the gifts of life, all the riches that we have received from loved ones, friends and acquaintances, all the abundance from the rich crop of the world's creativity: the bio-diversity of the planet on which we live, from the delicate life of flora or fauna, to the most dramatic natural landscape; the food sustenance harvested from the soil of mother earth; the joy of one's body meeting the hug of a loved one, or the warmth of a shower of water when cleansing the body; the comfort of clean clothes or newly laundered sheets; the ease of the temperature controlled space in which life is lived, and the kind gesture of a helper when all else appears unsound.

All of these gifts, all of these pleasures allow our hearts to expand and grow in the most natural of ways. So we experience love as compassion, kindness, patience, mercy, sincerity, peace, joy, forgiveness, gratitude and intimacy.

Then there is the giving: seeing the face of the children lighting up with innocent pleasure, the dawning of inspiration in the mind of a colleague you have stimulated, the eureka moment of surprise on your own face when an idea dawns after a time of interminable searching, the relief of a street-person smiling at the blessing of your help, and the joy of a loved friend in bliss at the ingenuity of your gift making. For all these tokens we give thanks. They make the other moments of controversy and challenge more tolerable. They signal and record that life is more appreciable after we have ached for a moment of meeting our heart's longing, or when travail hits and we feel shipwrecked by life's hurricanes.

In many ways these measures make up the lodestones of our lives, after which there are the deep furrows where ancient hatreds need to be translated into the gifts of love.

Imagine that you have two children before you who both need to acquire the knowledge of unconditional love and mature into emotional intelligence. One has been suffocated by so much receiving that it no longer knows how to give; a terrible anaesthesia permeates through its consciousness. The other has received so much brutality, and knows not how to give; your job is to teach giving and receiving with a bag of candy.

You start by offering candy to the spoilt child, who simply consumes whatever you give without the knowledge of its substance or the gift of its grace, then waits impatiently for more. Patiently pausing you turn to the brutalized child offering from the same bag of candy, but when this child receives the candy he or she immediately throws it into your face. You try again and again, only to receive the same seeming ingratitude.

Then in dismay you turn to the spoilt child and ask it to receive with thanks, but the child doesn't hear, and just consumes, so you try again, and again and again. As you make these further attempts to teach, the spoilt child becomes confused by your sustained approach and ceases immediately to consume, instead holding the candy.

Whilst this occurs the brutalized child watches suspiciously, and on turning back you offer another candy, which is again refused. But then the current shifts as the spoilt child offers its candy to the brutalized child who hesitatingly eats the candy, and so in a space of seconds a miracle is borne. Through patience and fortitude you have effectively taught the art of giving and receiving, and the confusion of ignorance and disdain is dispelled by the restoration of gratitude and appreciation.

When loving is true, and its quality is definable through the wings of its grace, the bruise of conditional love always smarts. When a token is expected in return for the initial gift, love becomes tainted. Conditional loving always ends up as ghastly. It always poisons the salve of unconditional love. Whereas, when gifts are given wanting no return, the Angelic chorus sing with uplifted heartfelt praise.

Love in its vibrational state is perceived not with the physical ears or eyes, love is perceived through the metaphysical, a sensing of more hallowed acclaim. Mystery seekers see it as the third eye, Christians see it as the Holy Spirit, and New Agers call it the Higher Self; whatever the vision, love is the intuitive gift of our hearts, clear as crystal and ancient as the stars. The knowledge of this joy rests in the secret chamber of our hearts, like an ancient memory of a pure water spring lying deep within our consciousness.

It haunts the movement of our more material selves, whose thirst for 'things' is never slaked.

TRUTH

Truth connects us with the crystal of transparency, which never allows falsehood to shine.

> *"Beauty is truth, truth is beauty – that is all*
> *Ye know on Earth, and all ye need to know."*

The poet John Keats write these lines at a time when the Industrial Revolution was beginning to ravage Mother Earth; reaping such havoc that she was never to be the same again, until now. For as the sacred Feminine is restored, we look to re-sacralize our planet and heal her womb.

Truth is that which is seen to be a supreme reality, that which has ultimate meaning as a value of existence. For where or what would we be without truth? The substance of truth, the very essence of truth, leaps like quanta through the aeons of time, leading us to a reminder of all that is essential, enduring and gives meaning. In an age where information technology abounds, where on a daily basis we peruse a huge flux of information through electronic mail, where would we be without the fundamentals that underpin the very fabric of our lives?

When we are called to the heart, we seek out its truth, because the heart is the organ of truth, and through it we yearn for that which is Sincere, and that which has Integrity. These qualities ripple through our hearts with the warm glow of assurance, and then tell our stories with pristine clarity, hope-filled innocence and resonating vigour.

It is with our hearts that we know the blueprint of truth, whereas our head leads us to the language of paradox and the rhetoric of duality. The head constantly questions: *"Shall I, shan't I, will I, won't I?"* Whereas the heart always knows, it simply and lovingly processes experience into intelligence and then into the knowledge of wisdom, like a divine cipher through which the secret chamber of the heart becomes coded as sincere.

Sincerity has a romantic meaning rooted in the Italian Renaissance. During this period, great works of art were created as a reflection of all that is most beautiful in mankind, and as an offering to the Divine. Notable personalities emerged that lifted their artistry to a remarkable degree of genius, one such being Michelangelo Buonarroti.

Michelangelo was commissioned by the council of Florence in 1501 to create the *David* statue, and chose to use marble, believing that the work already existed within the stone.

Executing such a powerful commission meant that great care needed to be taken, particularly as Pygmalion-like, the magic of form would be drawn from the block of stone. Marble is a dense metamorphic rock and so the sculptor's chisel needed to be delicately used - once the blade created an indentation that was not part of the artist's intention, the stone would be marred. If this occurred, the solution was to fill the gap with wax, and therefore once more the marble would appear unspoiled. This gave rise to the term 'Sincere' meaning 'without wax'.

If we create ourselves throughout our lives as flawlessly as possible, if we use compassion to heal our own damaged inner or outer being, we may also radiate a purity that is sincere, and find an integration of life's complexities.

Similarly the word Integrity is derived from the notion that if all parts or integers of self, namely the four essential bodies (physical, emotional, mental and spiritual) are integrated, we resonate with Integritas, and therefore we are sound and unimpaired. In the ancient world, this state was sought by all civilized beings, and was regarded as implicit within all behaviour that appeared grace-filled.

JOY

Joy derived from life is a creative edict, a supreme preoccupation, an experience that is the soul's delight, and yet instead, so many people reach for a pain-filled existence. So many of us hold emotional baggage from a past that prevents us from experiencing the joy filled moments of life. By living life through complex control dramas, through expectations about life, and judgements about others, we steep ourselves in unhappiness, and in stubbornly preventing ourselves from feeling joy, we forget that happiness is a decision not a condition.

Our heritage lies in the glory or roughness of past experience, our future lies in profound change, and the change that we are looking for lies in our visions. For if we think joyous thoughts life becomes joyous. It is through joy that all good things come, and as we learn to create ourselves anew, so our hearts call out for devotion.

If we see wisdom in this, we hold a key to the very substance of creation and we balance the duality of the creative force. This is the law of the Blue Planet Earth, the only planet of choice, for what is awakened consciousness but the ability to choose.

The question needs to be asked, what do you wish to become, for life is not a journey through which to discover self, but a means by which one can create oneself anew. Seek therefore, not to find out who you are, but who you wish to become, determining who you want to be in each moment, in each day, in each month, in each year. Utilize the highest choice to awaken your God-given gifts, for the lower choices of unhappiness and fear only produce confusion and dis-ease.

The highest thought is that which contains joy, the clearest words are those which speak truth, and the greatest feeling is that which we call love.

PIETY

Piety is a pathway to the garden of devotion, and in Ancient Rome the Goddess Pietas was associated with the duty shown to the Gods, Caesar and the State. The virtue of Pietas was held as a solemn condition alongside Gravitas and Dignity.

The true pathway of the pious is a garden created by love and eventually leading to God's paradise. But in order to purely love, we must surrender our negative ways of thinking—to feel an act of surrender not as a failure as in war, but as a supplication, as a means to let go and just love. By this action, by affirming that love is our priority, we embody the devotion of God.

Similarly, by walking the devotional pathway, by acknowledging love's importance in our lives, and our willingness to receive it, we literally call upon a higher power, yielding to the love that becomes a felicity in our lives.

Love erases fear, as light releases darkness, and as love shifts fear, God's message becomes clear, for this light is stronger than any trifling flicker. It is formed by the co-creation of God's infinite love and human intention to love forever. It is a shard of light suffused with all that is pure and good and true and real; it is *ALL THERE IS*.

HUMILITY

Humility is a peerless virtue. It is the lodestone of the spiritual temple, and of our lives. Its chief characteristic is that it expiates pride by healing it. When pride becomes rampant, an individual's behaviour radically diminishes the possibility of humility. Pride-filled action rests on a bed of conceit.

The act of humility in all truth is not the denial of one-self, but rather one of surrendering to a higher order. When we align with divine will and the devotion of service, we move into harmony with at-one-ment. We vibrate purely and live at a higher frequency.

The ancient ones who step forward at this time, those who have incarnated in the role of Avatar or Spiritual Leader, guide us to the knowledge that as we heal fear, and experience God's love bringing the word (the sound of intelligibility) full of grace and truth into our flesh and cleansing our cells, we move to a different trajectory, and our DNA vibrates at a higher frequency, creating greater atomic fusion.

This literally means our energy field radiates more light, and we glow with the energy of the Christos, the Christ light. Jesus said:

"He that believeth in me, the works that I do shall he do also, and greater works than these shall he do."

What do you think would happen if you radiated 90% atomic fusion?

Many Enlightened Ones or Bodhisattvas (Living Gods) are here at this time in the physical form of Mother Meera, Ammachi, HH the Dalai Lama and Sai Baba, and they are so powerful, they inspire us. Yet they do not have anything we do not have, other than they show us our potential. For they have love inside as we do; it's just that they have nothing else but love.

If we accept unconditional love in every aspect of our lives, if we dispel fearful thoughts, we become free by divine order. Thus our perspective utterly changes in the face of the miraculous, because it's easier to breathe in the sacred, and we are moved to our knees, humbled in the face of the Divine.

The term Mahatma, the name Gandhi was given, means 'one who breathes deeply'. When the inspirational fire of Pranayama moves through humankind, our physical membrane allows great power to exude, and we literally become suffused with the great Light. Jesus said:

"Blessed are the meek, for they shall inherit the kingdom of heaven."

Spirit Teachers, Mystics and Seers are revealing at this time that we are opening transpersonal Chakras that exist beyond the seven chakras of the physical body. Creative, evolutionary measures abound, for as we relinquish ourselves to spirit and the devotion of the soul, we move into the metaphysical domain of the non-local, and there we have five further Chakras.

The Eighth Chakra is the transition point, and may be perceived as a silver orb radiating into and from the unified field of light. This opens into the unity consciousness of divine love, defining all spiritual compassion and selflessness.

So the many allusions to this Chakra appear through the bounty of current data concerning the co-creative union we have with our brother and sisters, the planet and the universe. If you've missed the information don't worry, simply move onto your knees and tune into the hum in your heart, for the harmonic of unity consciousness moves through your energy system, into your energy grid through the eighth chakra and thence into your heart's chamber.

There you will feel softness, and a voice calling to you through the mists of time, reminding you of all that is fundamental to living love. Those that live love demonstrate this quality of consciousness, and become miraculous through their humility.

Humility means allowing God's light to shine through us. It's an invisible energy with visible effects. When we let go to truth, this charity, a charismatic force, breathes within us and seeks expression. So we allow our own light to shine brightly. This is not because of the need to use ego domination, but because we literally dare to live our heart's longing, our soul's note.

Simply, we are meant to be this way, to let our light shine, and as we allow the genuine innocence of our joy to the surface, we demonstrate the power of genuine humility. Truly, the light of whom we really are, both now and in the moment of becoming, shines forth as a beacon of magnificence, because our essence, our humility, our love resonates in freeness.

FAITH

Faith is a visionary force that allows us to open our hearts as we awaken to our souls. It is a belief in the fact that the Universe knows what it's doing, and as we yield to spirit and release the Ego, we realise that we are called forth to splendour.

Literally, we feel energy surging through the wholeness of our being that wasn't present before. This springs from the outer folds of infinity, just as it flows from the deeper recesses of our consciousness when we connect with the space of soul. This says: "yes!" and then we realize we are not alone, and we finally see a solution to the dilemma.

By the will of the Holy Spirit we feel the dawning of another day, which heralds a new life and one that is calm, cool and fully conscious. No recurring drama is seen. The day dawns after the storm with wreckage, but without shattering chaos, piercing anguish or scalding frustration. Rather we see where we came from and know where we rest.

Now, it is time to trust a force that moves the Universe, which is Faith. When we truly surrender to that which we are, we are taken care of with such assurance, the care of the best. Surrendering to God does not impede our creative power. This force is God's love. Love the essence, for His love is within us, and returning to it means we're returning to our truest nature.

When we surrender, we give up the attachments that have bound us to the fixation with outcome. When we give up attachment on the outside, the controlled desire for results, we live more completely on the inside. This creates true security, for the word se-cure means 'self-cure'.

Hope is restored and as we kneel at the altar of hope, it is faith that moves us to our veneration. For believing in God or the Source means we have help, a beneficence that shines through the chaos and reveals divine order. To have faith, to have belief and trust in this force is to move with the *source* of all creation, to become a Sorcerer. The Sorcerers and Wizards of old embodied this force, and travelled on it and with it, because it is present in all things.

Their power was derived from the *source*; not from blind faith but from visionary abilities, because they knew that the Cosmos knows what it is doing. They implicitly believed and trusted its power.

Faith is an awareness of the infinite field of unfolding possibility, the stream of wellbeing that flows through the Cosmos, from the inside, whereas our outer quests often require us to make a leap of faith, and fall into the workings of supreme trust in God's power. When we trust we float into this brilliant force, and the Angels carry us through divine succour. Any attempt to control interferes with the flow, whereas our willingness to relax and yield means it works on our behalf.

MERCY

Mercy is an essential attribute of divine love made human. Its grace evokes the truth of sovereign realms, as its emanation is of noble status. Its texture comes to us as though it were ambrosia from the Gods. Its action is the heartfelt experience of justice.

Shakespeare gave us a powerful teaching in the form of an initiation into mercy. It was written for Portia (the Goddess) to speak in *The Merchant of Venice*:

"The quality of mercy is not strained;
It droppeth as the gentle rain from heaven
Upon the place beneath. It is twice blessed;
It blesseth him that gives and him that takes.
'Tis mightiest in the mightiest; it becomes
The throned monarch better than his crown.
His sceptre shows the force of temporal power,
The attribute to awe and majesty,
Wherein doth sit the dread and fear of kings;
But mercy is above this sceptered sway.
It is enthroned in the hearts of Kings,
It is an attribute to God himself,
And earthly power doth then show likest God's
When mercy seasons justice."

Mercy is ultimate compassion. The experience of it literally takes our breath away, for it is from the elixir of prana that mercy emerges. When it arrives on earth it is as the gentle rain from heaven, for mercy is made from the tears of love, God's tears equally dispersed to the merciful as to the one who receives.

Shakespeare writes in his play *Measure for Measure*:

"…How would you be
If He, which is the top of judgement, should
But judge you as you are? O think on that,
And mercy then will breathe within your lips
Like man new made."

Compassion is one of the enchantments of the human experience. To feel its magic means that one must ask a paramount question of oneself: where does compassion lie in the heart? The conviction of compassion lies not in the observation, but more in the dispensation. If we believe that love is all there truly is, fear emerges as a mere illusion. Yet look at how many occasions we choose a defensive stroke rather than the bounty of compassion. Whether this be in thought or action, for thought is a living energy and so is received as a vibration before the action.

A client of mine told me this illuminating story about the power of thought as a living energy, and about the dispensing of compassion:

Rosemary's sister was driving home from a busy day at the office, one Friday evening in late autumn. Her journey was made more difficult by heavy, driving rain, and yet seemingly not perilous...at least, that is, until she was involved in a serial collision with many other vehicles on the major highway heading north out of the city.

As her car made impact with a heavy goods vehicle at between fifty or sixty miles (96 kms) per hour, the damage to her car was catastrophic, and her body was so badly injured that she died. Which is when she experienced a remarkable event.

As she died she felt herself floating above the wreckage of her car, moving towards a bright white light. There was no feeling of pain, merely a lightness of being, and a resignation to the unusual circumstance of floating above the carnage beneath. Then just as instantaneously there was the awareness of the passage of death, and an intense curiosity about a beam of light that appeared to be emerging from a car that was moving slowly, on the other side of the highway. As she looked more closely, she saw that the woman driving the car was praying for her body in the car wreckage.

This profoundly moved her and so she memorized the number registration of the compassionate woman's car. Then, realising that death was no longer beckoning, she returned to her body. A quaking feeling entered the whole of her consciousness that it was time to live and not to be released into paradise.

Six months later and almost fully recovered, after complex surgery and extensive hospitalisation, she entered the Vehicle Licensing and Registration Department of her local City Hall. Remembering the registration number of the car that had stopped, and the woman who had compassionately prayed for her, she obtained her home address and sent a bouquet of flowers to the merciful woman with an explanation of what had happened, and who she was. They have become dear, dear friends.

Today, there are many recorded experiences of NDE, of Near-Death-Experience, which are fascinating. Indeed, much literature has been written documenting the stories of thousands of people, and yet this tale must be one of the most extraordinary, it illuminates the sublime action of merciful compassion.

WISDOM

Wisdom is a grace gained after a time of heightened experience, competent understanding and refined knowledge.

"Those who know others are wise,
Those who know themselves are enlightened"
– LEONARDO DA VINCI

When experience becomes embodied, when the very essence of knowing has had time to seep into our whole physical presence, into the core of our cells, it forms an oasis of emotional intelligence. Then, and only then may we drink the balm quenching waters of wisdom.

Thus a balance between the opposites of thought and feeling is established; the first being accomplished by experiential comprehension, and the second being calibrated by the apprehension of finer feeling. You see, without the fusion of head and heart working together there is no wisdom. To reform the severed connection between body and mind is the awakening of embodied truth. For without clear intention and loving compassion there is no sacred conduit along which wisdom may flow.

The ancients believed that the source of all wisdom was found at a meeting within us, of two conduits: the axis mundi and the anima mundi. In the deepest part of this conjunction is a reflection of the very essence of whom we are. Wise, serene and powerful beyond measure, this meeting crosses the realm of the heart, the lodestone from which all love pours. This is where the icon of the Cross was created; but not as a nexus of bitter sacrifice — rather as a rendezvous of glorified service.

Both Axes are formed like the signpost of life itself. Both are partners in a dynamic and exciting dance of opposites, for in their embrace both matter and consciousness reach a point where each is informed and enhanced by the other. This is where mind and body correlate into the mystery of spirit, because this is where the heart and brain, the literal and the metaphoric, the proven and the unproven, the seen and the unseen meet to create an incandescence of truth.

The Axis Mundi holds a key to our vertical nature, the heart and the brain, the body and the mind, the gravity of the earthly magnetic matter and the heavenly loftiness of the electrical spirit.

To strengthen this Axis means we must organize the core principles of the self. For these polarities reflect the conditions of the female and male energies, the yin and the yang, the being and the doing, the thinking and the feeling, the soma and the psyche, the profane and the sacred, the dark and light, the earth and the heavens, the freedom and the effort. In acknowledging these forces, we become anchored in the core identity of our self, the I AM.

The pronoun 'I' commands the spine, and therefore the Pranic cord. This is the I AM Presence that produces a full recognition of our sovereignty in the attainment of being a healthy soul. With this knowledge our experience is initiated in the conviction of love, and confirmed in devotion to God.

The Anima Mundi vitalizes the horizontal nature of our force. It is formed by and from the animating principle of the Universe, created by God's breath. At one and the same time the Anima arises from and creates the soul of the Cosmos.

In the Bible's Book of Genesis, we see particular mention of the Anima Mundi, for it is written that God breathed into the nostrils of man the breath of life, and man became a living soul.

This invigorating zephyr of well-being is the force that is the Source. This is the energy that permeates the consciousness of all living things on earth and elsewhere, and gives the life that they have. This is the force that the ancient Magicians knew of, and which formed them as Sorcerers, for their knowledge arose from the Source, and then tuned them back in, for the creation of great magic.

This is the *inspiration* of our own breath, the great breathing in. For to be *sound in heart* means we need to be alive with the pulse of life, with the breath of the holy wind. Inspiration is a derivative of this force, for to be inspired is to be in connection with the animating principle of the universe: *inspirare* is to breathe in spirit, and to be in connection with the Divine, the Morphogenetic Field.

To heal the mind and the body, to allow the very fermentation of wisdom to occur, we need a union of both the Axis & Anima Mundi. As these conduits connect, an integration of Divine proportion takes place. For, just as we fully come to know self by penetrating the shadow of the underworld — our unconscious self — we then consciously commit to the reconstitution of our souls.

This is reflected in the Crucifixion of the Christ. For when we truly know ourselves in the balance between truth and illusion, when we can truly allow the ego to die in the knowledge of the fact that we are of spirit, we resurrect and begin to glimpse the heavenly route to a higher consciousness, the pathway to the possibility of Ascension.

The longitudinal and latitudinal shafts of light that open to us through an awareness of these wisdom conduits further lead us to an unfolding of events at the highest level, for the good of ourselves and for the ultimate good of all. In many ways we do not need to do anything complex, we simply need to show up with a smile on our face.

LOYALTY

Loyalty is created on the anvil of devotion. To be loyal is to be faithful to a person or cause. It is the seal of honour itself, it is the adhesion that allows the devotional pathway to stay consistent, to stay practiced. Without loyalty there is disconnection from the path, there is dissipation into the selfishness of the ego, and any connection with spirit, with the vital essence of life is lost.

Plato is reported to have said that only a man who is just can be loyal, and that loyalty is an aspect of genuine philosophy. The word philosophy is derived from Greek and means 'a lover of wisdom', just as the Goddess Sophia was a symbol for the love of wisdom. Therefore, a loyal philosopher was seen to woo the Goddess to revelation, to be a radiance of that wisdom which is love.

When we lack resolve, when we are moved from our path by a quaking tremor of life, when we feel doubt seizing our experience of goodness, it is nourishing to reach out for poetry rich in spiritual aphorisms. Poetry contains heightened states of metaphor, and can teach us to reconnect with the language of hope.

Through the language of the heart, we become realigned with the light of the essence that has seemingly diminished. Here is a poem that can stimulate remembering honour when we feel a lack of loyalty:

I am what I am.
Loyalty is my essence, and my seal of honour.
Therefore, having faith in the beauty within me, I develop trust.
In softness I have strength.
In silence I walk with the Gods.
In peace I understand myself and the world.
In conflict I walk away, as in detachment I am free.
In respecting all living things I respect myself.
In dedication I honour the courage that is within me.
In eternity I have compassion for the nature of all things.
In unconditional love I accept the evolution of other beings.

– ANON

COURAGE

Courage is the virtue of certainty, even in the face of the uncertain. Courage is an upholding of the right cause when no end is in sight, and without promise of reward. Courage is the will to muster on, even if injury or defeat may be the outcome.

Schopenhauer suggested that:

> *"Every truth passes through three stages before it is recognized. In the first, it is ridiculed. In the second, it is opposed. In the third, it is regarded as self-evident."*

Those who have proclaimed their truth by returning to the power of love have faced ordeals. As spiritual warriors we have faced confirmed reticence, the ridicule of dismissal, the brandishing of the Ego from those who are committed to a love of power, and possibly the loss of those who once succoured us.

God's message tells us that the awakening of this era is more than universal, and every mind receives it. It's just that some minds choose not to open themselves to the very call of their hearts, and as difficult as this may be, if we are called, we must review their choice compassionately.

Tests of faith and courage confirm whom we are as vessels for the Holy Spirit, whilst we perform the role of mid-wife to the birth of a new paradigm. Our courage enlightens our way, with the light of the knowledge that when we think and feel with love, we self-actualize God. When this is so we become co-creators in the ultimate power, which is love.

Any other choice would be to commit perjury in the face of the Divine, and so our courage provides us with fortitude and stamina, and our will shines.

JUSTICE

The essence of Justice lies not within judgement, but within the profound recognition of the harmony that exists at the heart of natural order. The manifestation of justice occurs through the conceptual attitudes of human beings with regard to moral rightness. In this we may see justice as an instinctual, behavioural trait directed by an innate sense of fairness.

In 2003 at Emory University in Georgia, studies involving Capuchin monkeys led to the surprising conclusion that cooperative monkeys show the same degree of 'inequality aversion' that most human beings do.

Justice is the ability to say "No!" when no is needed. When inequality reigns, when a soul is denied, when inequity is rife, when power is misused, when a heart is attacked, when lack of compassion is apparent, when abuse is determined, when the name of love is vilified or grace reviled, we have the right to say a very loud and palpable "No!"

This does not mean we become creatures of violence or defence. Our core power lies in being responsive and not reactive. Therefore, defence, blame, accusation, anger and paranoia are all indications of a lack of love, a fear of love, and a resistance to be free. Resistance is the challenge resting in the fact that aggression has become common currency in our world, and in order to allow the heart to sound, in order to love as purely as we can, we must surrender the old ways of thinking and doing.

Yet surrender is challenging for most of us because we are taught that it is commensurate with failing. Please see true surrender as love tempering violence, as an agent of change. This is when justice becomes a lover of harmony.

Fundamentally JUST NESS is the instrument by which all this is maintained. It is the conviction that lies in the attainment of beauty and fairness of love, your love, God's love. It is the central belief that captivates the joy of life, and which creates personal magnetism.

The magnet is the voice of your freedom counsellor. This is your own highly personalised emotional GPS system, or your individualized satellite-navigation system. This is your heart plumbing its depths and magnetically pointing to your higher self, just as a compass moves to the North.

When the compass moves, can you be faithless to be trustworthy? Can you be firm in your own heartfelt truth and therefore disappoint another human being if necessary? Can you bear the thousand natural shocks that flesh is heir to, or the slings and arrows of outrageous fortune, and yet not betray your own soul, your own truth, your own love? Can you say "No!" after years of complicity with "Yes"?

When we surrender to our personal destiny, God's will takes over and directs us. If we let go, if we yield or surrender, we discover a new perception. We awaken from the nightmare of thinking ourselves weak and unloved, and accept that the power of the universe is within us, and will guide us. This is when the soul becomes victorious. This is when one of the sacred Beatitudes spoken by the Master Jesus can be used to teach our devotional way, for:

"Blessed are they that do hunger and thirst after righteousness, for they shall be filled."

VICTORY

Victory means peace, and peace is an assignation with the Divine. Conversely, in the secular world, the word victory applies to the resolution of an act of warfare conjuring strong feelings of elation usually resulting in victorious cries, dances, parades and ceremonies; whereas in the sacred context victory is associated with peace and joy arising from the completion of a soul's task.

Thus, incarnating souls bring lessons to be learned, karma to be healed, spirit endeavours to be wrought from the breath of life and the wisdom of the heart.

Victory creates a radical commitment to a new way of being, which begins with practice and discipline formulated by meditation and prayer, allowing the development of spiritual muscle. Honed in the soul's gym, we become embodied with such strength that we defy the ego's voice and truly inherit the victorious kingdom of heaven, not *there* but here.

Spiritual victory is not about becoming more complex from a metaphysical perspective or of acquiring psychic technology by reading the latest book; rather it is a question of becoming simpler and of evolving through the heart's truth. The soul's gym uses the work of Meditation (listening to God) and Prayer (speaking to God) as its major trainers. These eternal compasses are designed to strengthen our spiritual conviction, to develop the hardware of our DNA.

Through exercise the Divine permeates deeper into our being, and as we bring our souls fully into our physical body, we have the chance to truly experience spiritual alchemy. Conversely, if the ego dashes our souls from our bodies, our thinking becomes confused, our feelings bridle in utter chaos. What changes when we bring our souls back is not simply what we do, but more importantly who we become.

Meditation and prayer discipline our mental, emotional and physical bodies; they allow us to configure greater peace, and radiate greater stillness. You see in the stillness of meditation we find the infinity of the soul, which we are led to believe is within us, whereas truly we are within soul. This source of soul is infinite energy. This force of being focuses life within the unified field of unfolding possibility. This is simply complete wellbeing.

When we are aware of this source, God and Godly emissaries move through us. When we are in connection with the source, the monkey-chatter of the ego's voice ceases to control us, and instead we hear the still small voice within, soothing our preoccupation with the battle of life, for in truth no victory lies.

Spiritually victorious human beings may be in essence fit, and yet are not people who rush around; more so they are people around which a lot gets done. We see emanating from their behaviour a stillness that is their route to power.

Observe the life of two extraordinary beings: President Clinton (post Lewinski-gate) moving effortlessly as a Peace Ambassador and Sovereign all over the planet, using his experience of the earth as his kingdom. Each political move he makes, each word he utters has gravitas and integrity. These qualities were honed through desperate circumstances, and gave rise to his unique intelligence. The note of this *sound heart* is evoked in statements like:

> *"It does not require a majority to prevail, but rather a tireless minority keen to set brush fires in people's minds."*

Similarly, Mahatma Ghandi who assisted in the liberation of the Indian people from British Sovereignty, not by doing, but rather by being within the conviction of non-violence and using love as a crown of victory. Gandhi said:

> *"Be the change you want to see in the world. For first they will ignore you, then they will laugh at you, then they will fight you, and then you will win."*

Victory is soul both ascending and descending in force. It is both male and female verities bonding within the entity of soul. Thus we lighten up and incarnate through the whole of our body in true union with God.

In Conclusion...

I'm concluding this chapter with a meditation, for when peace reigns, balanced in the holy space where ancient hatred is dispelled by present love, the heart's chamber rings with the strength of a new bell, drawing us to worship, drawing us to venerate the light of our power.

The light, the manifestation of all that is good about us can always be rekindled through meditation, tuning us to the *source*, and when we sound our note and tune our hearts and souls, all profoundly appears as being well.

When we truly know that love from the *source* is infinite, we re-source it more easily, for there is enough abundance for everybody. What we give to others is brought back a thousand-fold, and so we understand paradise.

When we arrive at heaven's gate it is so much easier to bless than to condemn others through judgement.

Heaven's Gate Meditation

- Make sure you have Silence, Solitude and Stillness.
- Move to your Sacred Space and switch on Voicemail, so that you won't be disturbed.
- Light a candle and burn some incense to cleanse and soothe the atmosphere
- Find a chair or cushion on which you feel your spine is comfortably aligned, and your body weight balanced. Place your hands separately on your lap or knees, and place your fingers into a Mudra; such as forefinger and thumb together. This will unite powerful energies within your physique and thence within the whole energy field.
- Imagine the Pranic Cord moving through your spine generating from your heart: see a laser beam of light shining through your spine, and chose a colour for it, or imagine it is the pure white light of the source.
- See the Pranic cord moving down through the base of your spine, and through the various levels beneath you until you reach bedrock. Once there, anchor the cord of light into Mother Earth, and notice how you feel completely held by her force, as a force of unconditional love, compassionately supporting your weight and gravity. Ask her for a gift, a blessing, or a token and siphon that force up through the varying levels up into your body
- Move the cord of light back into your heart, and then past the seat of your soul (your heart's chamber) through the top of your spine and off into Father Heaven. See the cord of light move to your favourite star in the Heavens, and if you don't know which it is, choose one as this could be a planetary home. Venus is the brightest star in the night's sky and one that benignly overshadows this work, as Venus is the Planet of Love.
- Feel breath as the source. Breathe all the breath out of your body. Then wait a moment before you breathe in Life Force. When you breathe in, see the breath as light or colour moving through your body, and like an elevator moving down inside your spine. Breathe wide and deep with the power of Chi, and breathe out on AH... the heart vowel.

If you wish continue this 7 times, and then…

- Visualise a Violet Five Pointed Star shielding the front of your Heart Chakra, about seven inches (17 ctmtrs) in size. Breath in, and as you sound out on AH, spin the Star in a counter-clockwise direction.
- Visualise a Violet Pointed Star shielding the rear of your Heart Chakra, again seven inches (17 ctmtrs) in size, and on the next breath in, and as you sound AH, spin the Star in a clockwise direction. We'll do this together three times on AH
- These Stars protect your Heart Chakra, stimulate Pranayama in this area of your energy field, and like a Talisman they will open your heart's secret chamber.
- Sound AH twice more and then rest. Observe the heightened sensations within your body. Remember the intuitions you receive. Record the feeling that your Heart has opened a gate to heaven.
- Sound OM to seal your field, and as you enchant feel the extraordinary sensitivity of your physical presence.
- Feel yourself soaking in soul……OM

CHAPTER THREE

Heart Love

Our forefathers had civilization inside them,
the wildness was outside.
We live in the civilization they created,
and within us wildness lingers.
What they dreamed we live,
and what they lived we dream.
– WALT WHITMAN

We are energy, evolving through the momentum of weight, space and time, and the velocity of this force, the instrument with which we live our outer lives, accelerates our passage, and yet if not consciously respected can dangerously move us away from the innermost truth of our souls. Thereby confusion reigns. Our civilized essence revealed through love, honesty, beauty, grace and truth becomes juxtaposed with the wildness of the ego existing in negativity, separation, competition, fear, possession and strife. Furthermore the Ego, and its fixation with 'doing', creates an incessant chatter in our heads. For the Ego is always threatened by the stillness of essence, in retaliation it creates several voices that self-righteously squabble: *"Shall I, shan't I, will I, won't I"* or *"You're not very good"* or *"How dare she!"*

The truth of the soul is made opaque by the noise of this din, and so doubt and confusion come to blunt our purpose and subjugate our spirit. Lamentably this has been long in happening; Renaissance history shows us this, and Shakespeare warned us thus:

"Our doubts are traitors,
And make us lose the good we oft might win,
By fearing the attempt."

Yet even when the Ego takes hostage of our soul, the movement and symphony of the Universe unerringly directs us to the ultimate force of love. Ever benign, the heart as the seat of the soul waits patiently, sometimes somnolent like 'sleeping beauty' waiting for her prince; waiting till we actively choose to awaken the heart's chamber, through the release of pain and the gift of love. For 'patience like a monument' always yields to the wait; waiting for her Prince to evolve courage, and now is the Prince's time. Now doubt must be released to the void from whence it came. Now like a rampant truth-filled lover, it is time for that kiss.

Albert Einstein, a lover of science and mysticism, woke us at the beginning of the twentieth century with his discovery of the law of relativity, and we moved into the age of atomic fusion. But this potential gave vent, not just to the creation of atomic fuel, it also split the planet's body.

Nature Is De-Sacralized

Truth be told, the Romantic Movement during the eighteenth century had already warned us. Their caveat appeared as they witnessed Mother Nature being ripped apart by the new machines during the onset of the industrial revolution. The force of science coupled with the ravaging desire of the ego, defined through the might of the machine, de-sacralized nature.

William Blake wrote:

> *"I wander thro' each charter'd street,*
> *Near where the charter'd Thames does flow,*
> *And mark in every face I meet*
> *Marks of weakness, marks of woe.*
>
> *In every cry of every Man,*
> *In every infant's cry of fear,*
> *In every voice, in every ban*
> *The mind-forg'd manacles I hear.*

Einstein, one of the greatest minds of the twentieth century, knew this and pledged concerns, for he saw the potential disassociation, as he wrote: *"The intuitive mind is a sacred gift, the rational mind a faithful servant. We have created a society that honours the servant and has forgotten the gift."*

Restoring Balance

Our work in *The Heart's Note* is a return to balance, to awaken the heart's voice and to claim the vital promise of the heart's action in our new lives. For we are not what we were, but are what we are becoming.

Weighing the heart substantiates a gift of integration and truth. Sounding the heart with words of inspiration and grace opens the secret chamber of the heart. Loving the heart steadfastly increases its essence and power. Divining the heart pelts the heart with petals of tenderness and humility, sanctifying its existence. Honouring the miracle of the heart with compassion, integrity and respect dispels the wilderness of the shadow. Moving our spirits by 'heart dowsing' 3D life conjures belief, faith and trust.

This confirms the heart's status in the world, for make no mistake this is the age of the heart. This is the time for the heart as a prime integrator of consciousness to trigger in all of us a new level of consciousness. For the heart's empathy and compassion will lead us to unity consciousness, enabling all of us to acknowledge our species as *We* rather than that of the *I*. In living this potential we become what was intended millennia ago – the truth that we are divine beings.

Feeling Synergy through Entrainment

When we awaken our hearts, we automatically move into the miracle of synergy. When we transform the ego's singularity into unity with the soul, a powerful entrainment is borne.

During the seventeenth century, many eminent Europeans explored human intelligence through an era known as the age of enlightenment. Many fine contributions were made to the advancement of modern science, and one such invention originated from Christian Huygens.

Huygens became successful through his creation of the pendulum clock, a collection of which he kept in his study. One day, to his utter astonishment he found all the clocks moving in coherence; literally they were all oscillating through the same movement, which had happened even though he had begun their movement at different intervals of time.

Determined to unsettle this, he re-started the pendulums, moving them at different periods. However, once again he found all the clocks moved back into synchrony. Further observation proved that the largest of the pendulums, the one with the strongest rhythm, was pulling the other smaller pendulums into synergy with it. Astounded, he continued to explore the natural world for this phenomenon, and saw that it extended throughout much of life; the enormity of this discovery has become known as the science of Entrainment.

To observe further in human behaviour, see the effects of entrainment in times of profound societal trauma, such as 9/11. Or, the waves of compassion that moved through thousands of people at the death of Diana, and at the Darshan given by Ammachi, the hugging saint, who evokes the Divine Mother through the whole of her being.

David McClelland, a psychologist at Harvard University conducted an experiment in the 1980s in which he showed a group of students a film of Mother Teresa of Calcutta. Surely, we all felt Mother Teresa to be an embodiment of love, care and compassion moving through large numbers of poor or destitute people. However, when the group had finished watching the film, tests showed that there had been a significant rise in the saliva antibody IgA, effecting change in the immune system of each person's body.

You see, loving through the heart means that when our bodies, minds and souls are entrained, all our organs move into harmony or synchronization, and when we sense this synergy we literally think and feel better. This is felt through our four bodies ~ the physical, emotional, mental and spiritual ~ all move to optimum efficiency, for the heart is the strongest biological pendulum in the body, drawing through entrainment, all other organs to it.

Of course, we experience this most when we are in heightened states of emotion: when we love - admiration, awe, and exquisite joy flood through our beings, enveloping our brains and hearts in their movement to coherence, and producing a synergy that creates waves of force which amplify intuition and intimacy - we feel the immensity of life pouring through us.

Observe those personal moments in your life when you have been moved by profound stimuli, whether this be a wonderful piece of music, an amazing sunset, an awe-inspiring natural landscape, the beautiful innocence of a child, or a lover's embrace. In these moments we cascade into a knowing that is utterly at one with self. In these points of truth we are 'in sync' with ourselves, and crescendo into a synergy of the divine symphony. This can be known as the passion of compassion.

The great poet Gerard Manley Hopkins beautifully caught this moment of bliss in a poem he wrote entitled *The Windhover*:

I caught this morning morning's minion, king-
　dom of daylight's dauphin, dapple~dawn~drawn Falcon, in his riding
　　Of the level underneath him steady air, and striding
High there, how he rung upon the rein of a wimpling wing
In his ecstasy! then off, off forth on swing,
　As a skate's heel sweeps smooth on a bow~bend: the hurl
　and gliding
　　Rebuffed the big wind. My heart in hiding
Stirred for a bird, the achieve of, the mastery of the thing!

The ramifications of these exquisite moments are myriad, for entrainment allows us to reach a peak experience, when we attain our full functioning capacity as pulsating soul beings. And being of this vibration means our electro-magnetic field expands, our ability to accommodate more light increases, and we experience that our DNA is encoded with radical shifts of biological growth, enhancing the very biography of our lives.

The preamble to these conditions must be the healing of the emotional body, and its interface with our meta-physicality. The tuition and the in-tuition of emotional intelligence heals our shadow, and if we cannot see this occurring, because the unconscious restraint of unexplored conflict will not allow full integration to take place, we must labour to find freedom.

Conflicts bring with them corrupted energies that fill us and weigh down our potential to lighten up, to become en-lightened. Yet conversely, when we are alight through healing, each Chakra expands its force and our energy field exudes fuller light. Magically this increases our ability to receive inspiration, developing our energetic bandwidth, expanding our oracular consciousness, producing wave after wave of loving compassion, and the ability to co-create the future.

> "The heart's electromagnetic field is by far the most powerful produced by the body; it's approximately five thousand times greater in strength than the field produced by the brain. The heart's field not only permeates every cell in the body but also radiates outside of us; it can be measured up to eight to ten feet away with sensitive detectors called magnetometers."
> — FROM THE THE HEARTMATH SOLUTION, BY DOC CHILDRE AND HOWARD MARTIN.

To develop the synergy we seek, to make coherent the brain and the heart, *Sound* as a building block of creation may be used through our own voice. *Sound* literally stops the monkey-chatter of non-specified thought, for when our voice creates certain frequencies, the right and left hemispheres of the brain become harmonized, and we seep into serenity with the symphony of the creative eternal. Thus, *Sound* mirrors the heart's nature to entrain our whole biology. Try the Sonic Meditation on the following page.

Chakra Meditation To Open Love
Through The Sound Of The Cosmos

- Move into your Sacred Space, and make sure you are not disturbed.
- Light a candle and burn incense to create renewed healing in this peaceful environment.
- Remember to switch on voicemail, communicate your need for Silence, Solitude and Stillness to those with whom you live, or simply close the door for privacy in this sacred space, where you feel you can freely create sound.
- Find a comfortable chair on which to sit, and earth your body with your feet on the floor removing your shoes. Loosen tight clothing and sit with your spine aligned. Try not to use the back of the chair, as leaning in this fashion can compromise your ease of breath, by moving your spine from its alignment. Make sure your feet are on the floor with shoes off, and place your hands comfortably on your lap with your fingers in a Mudra (a spiritual gesture as a seal of authenticity ~ bringing your thumb and forefinger together connects the sun and moon energies throughout your body).
- Feel your spine reflecting the great I AM THAT I AM presence through its fully aligned status. Visualize the Pranic Cord as a laser beam of light shining through the whole of your spine. This may be a colour of your own choosing, or visualize gold as an Angelic vibration connecting with your heart chakra.
- Visualise the Pranic cord moving down through the whole of your spine, and the levels of the earth's surface, the soil, clay, stone and rock, finally into bedrock. See the cord anchor into Mother Earth, and notice how magnetic gravity draws you into the womb of the Divine Mother. Then bring the cord up, siphoning the flow of Divine Mother's energy, up through the successive levels of rock, stone, clay and soil, reversing the process you used earlier, and visualize the Pranic Cord moving upwards through the earth, through the building, then through the whole of your spine, and the upper floors of the building in which you are placed. See the cord moving into Father Heaven's Universe, and if you know it, to your own cosmic home. If you are unaware of this, see the cord travel to the Planet Venus, the Goddess of love. Venus is the brightest star in the sky, and particularly serves the vibration of this heart work.
- Move through your body to the Base Chakra, seeing a Red Disc three to four inches (10 cms) outside your body, and beneath your

perineum. Let your breath empty, and then breathe in wide and deep (moving your rib cage and upper abdomen) seeing the breath as a light force filling your whole body. Then sound the vowel AW through the Red Disc, and as you tone, spin the disc in a clockwise direction for the masculine vector, or a counter-clockwise if you are female. Do this three times on a pitch that is coherent with this part of your body, and you will activate this Chakra which is responsible for all earth-ing processes, concerning your identity and your power in the world. This Chakra usually activates during the first year or eighteen months of life.

- When complete with the process of spinning the Base Chakra, move to the Second Chakra, seeing an Orange Disc hovering before and behind your sexual identity centre or sacrum. Breathe out, and when fully empty breathe in wide and deep. Sound OO and spin the Orange Chakra. Do this three times extending the breath through the OO, and feel a pitch that is coherent with this part of your body. Spin the disc in a manner that corresponds with your gender as mentioned before. This Chakra signifies core qualities to do with our relationship processes, and usually activates during the two to three year old period of life experience. PAUSE.

- Move to the Third Chakra, seeing a Yellow Disc hovering before and behind your solar plexus. In a second breathe out, and when empty breathe in wide and deep to sound OH on a pitch that is coherent with this part of your body. Do this three times spinning the disc, and notice the effect on your body. This Chakra signifies core qualities to do with the development of your will, both loss and gain through the emotional body. It usually activates during the four to six year old process of life experience.

- Move to your Heart Chakra where we will repeat the process. However, this Chakra sound is AH, toned on a pitch that intuitively relates to this part of the body. The colour of the Chakra is Green. Pause when you've toned this Chakra three times, and notice all four Chakras spinning. The Heart Chakra activates during the seven to nine year old period, and is related to self-knowledge. Once we've toned three times, observe how extraordinary your energy feels. It is at this stage of the meditation that people often experience Divine transmission. PAUSE.

- Move to the fifth Chakra in your throat. The colour will be light Blue. Breathe out all the breath within. Wait a moment and then when you feel the need to breath, breathe wide and deep and tone the vowel AY through your throat, using an intuitively placed pitch for this location. The Throat Chakra is mystically known as the entry point and leaving point of the soul. For this reason it is extremely sensitive, and so observe the subtle responses that take place within you. This Chakra usually activates during the ten to thirteen year old period of life and signifies energies associated with self-expression.

- Move to the forehead, the colour of this Chakra is Indigo, and see a disc both before and behind. The sound to use is I. Spin the disc three times and when finished pause to feel the force. This Chakra activates during the fourteen to sixteen year old period of life experience, and is associated with the objectivity of choice. This time is a period for sorting out life's priorities. Also, the Forehead Chakra is the locus of the vestigial third eye, a centre of visionary thought and increased intuition.

- And then move to the Crown Chakra, and its colour Violet, and exists three or four inches (9 cm), above the top of your head. After you have explored the breath, breathing wide and deep, spin the Chakra three times toning EE. You will feel a gateway open within the inner and outer consciousness. This creates sensitivity for all feeling associated with the spirit of life.

- When you have toned EE pause, reflect on each of the seven chakras spinning and humming the frequency you have created. Opening these powerful data-bases opens us to our at-one-ment. You will feel each chakra revolving individually, as well as being in a unified state. Observe how the chakras appear along your pranic cord, radiant, serene and as spinning vortices. Observe this magic. Indeed, you may even feel a larger, more exquisite presence around your energy field. For when we open the first seven chakras through these sonic chambers, we open celestial portals through which the body of sound is inspired to act as powerful sonic bells throughout the cosmos. These bells are invitations to those forces of the Cosmos that correspond most with the coherence of love. The Angels, Elementals, Ancient Ones, and the Holy Spirit ~ those beings that correspond wholeheartedly with the Love-Light circuitry.

- Now, imagine a silver orb twelve inches (30cm) above your head, about seven inches (17cm) in diameter. Take a breath wide and deep into your relaxed being and tone HEE. This time see the HEE revolving the SILVER ORB as your Eighth Chakra ~ this is the chakra of unity consciousness, and is the first transpersonal chakra most particularly activated at this time of transcendent evolution. In human terms the eighth chakra is the gateway to the dawning of Aquarius, and so see the symbol for infinity placed above the spinning chakra.

- Imagine your energy field is surrounded by a veil of golden light protecting your force. Then be still, and receive the ministrations of Love from the Cosmos. In these moments we remember who we truly are. We remember Love untarnished. We feel unmarked by the contaminations of the world and free from the conceit of our Ego. We sense ourselves to be soaking in a holy instant, where nothing at all matters other than what we 'be'. For only when we move aside from the Ego's account of us can we truly feel what we are, and what we are to be is whole, because whom we are is Holy. When we rest in this sacred moment, we rest in the Source, remembering that in fact we never left, we simply fell asleep.
- Awakening from this Lethe means we re-member the Source and become Sorcerers again. We awaken to our true self, freeing us from the nightmare of the material world, and so we become aligned with the mind of God. Our souls are extensions of this mind, and as such our truth is that we are Divine. As we open our hearts completely to this power, both with *GOD* and the *WE* of unity consciousness, our beings become conduits for the miraculous.
- In moments such as these, when we truly open our hearts to God, it is important to seal the door of remembering with a prayer - a prayer filled with love, like the one below. Love is the flowing circuitry that is the creation of the Cosmos, created through a thought of well-being arising from the mind of God.
- Let us feel the vastness of this infinite love, embracing us as children. Let us feel the eternal light within us, because God put it there. Let us invoke our light, because in the presence of light the darkness disappears.

A Prayer To Seal
The Door Of Remembrance

Dear God,

You are always a thing of beauty in my eyes, a word of love in my ears, a sense of glory in my body, a thought of joy in my mind, and a wave of compassion in my heart.

Please let me remember the sacred lineage of my being, as it in my soul's force.

Please let me bring forth my light into the world, and not diminish my power.

Please let me proclaim the truth of my spirit, as though it were as sweet as Angels' song.

Thank you dear God.

So let it be.

Amen

The Dawning Of Aquarius

As Aquarius dawns the eighth Chakra opens, and so we begin to activate the five Chakras of our trans-personal awareness, completing the octave of our personality-based consciousness. The eight Chakra is a tremendously powerful portal for our souls, for their elevation and ascension. For through this silver orb we move from personal fulfilment to unity consciousness, from the 'I' to the 'We'.

Evolving thus allows our return to the full belief in pneuma as the psyche of the soul, the Source of infinitely unfolding well-being that is the Universe. And so we move beyond the limitations of our individual human perception, recognizing that we are not 'alone' but 'all-one'.

Unity consciousness means that we fully recognize we are co-creating the consciousness of our lives, and our world together. When waking to the awareness of this we aspire to cosmic consciousness, we connect with the ability to experience the whole of heaven through the diversity of our being. From the seeming mortality of our flesh, we transcend to pure spirit. From the local, we move to the non-local. From the reintegration of our mind, heart and spirit, we truly feel the potential of the kingdom of love, emanating from and through all souls. For to love another, is to see the face of God.

A Vision Of God's Face

When God shows His face it is always through the illuminating creation of love, just as it was for Moses during his forty-day vigil whilst receiving the Ten Commandments. The bible says that Moses' face shone as he left the presence of God, and that God showed His face through the light of the burning bush. These lights were the aura or halo of the sacred made manifest. These lights signified the arousal of the eighth Chakra (or Halo) as an awakening of divine light.

At this time, like Angels with wings of light, a new heart pulses within us, and Aquarius dawns within the cosmology of our souls. Our first full witness of Aquarius was on January 23rd 1997, when the Age of Aquarius was cosmically ushered in by a unique star configuration of celestial grandeur. God's evolving intention was seen as a perfectly formed Star of David in the heavens, a six-pointed star symbolizing the archetypal union of opposites created by the joining of two equilateral triangles. The Star represents the masculine and feminine elements moving into a divine union as a sacred marriage.

In the ancient world this was known as the 'Hieros Gamos' (taken from the Greek and meaning holy wedding), when the God and Goddess elements become linked in sexual intercourse. The rituals surrounding HG permeate through most of the world's ancient cultures. For example, in Kabbala the HG is seen as a HexaGram representing a man and woman in intimate embrace, and as an icon was secreted in the Arc of the Covenant alongside the Ten Commandments.

Since 'sacred union' is the source of all life on our planet, the six-pointed star uniting the archetypal male and female has long been acknowledged as a model for earthly balance and celestial integration. Indeed, medieval Alchemists called the six-pointed Star the 'philosophers stone'. The Magi or Alchemists added a tiny dot to the upper right hand point of the Star to signify the presence of God and the guidance of the Holy Spirit. The Star represented the heart of the entire living Cosmos, freshly revitalized as a new heart, and one that loves into creation the energies of equality, communion and co-creativity.

Core Tools For The Heart's Note

To live with the awareness of this sacred union within us is to function from the prism of the heart at the core of life. To dowse with our heart, to breathe our heart's choice, to sound our heart's note, to shape our destiny with the heart's voice is a profound act. For the truth is that you need no one else to create your dream of the kingdom of heaven here on earth –just as breathing is a decision when feeling flushed with pain, just as happiness is a decision when feeling the depths of despair, just as love can be the decision when faced by unconscionable fear. For now and until the end of time, happiness is a decision and not just a condition, for the key to happiness is the way of love, and love withheld is the key to pain.

When a decision is honed we simply need to practise keeping thought steady and true: the main thing is to keep the main thing, the main thing. For if thought creates reality, the only truly intelligent force existing is when thought is linked with purpose.

Practise appreciation, and you will become appreciative. Practise non-judgement, and you will become non-judgemental. Practise forgiveness, and you will be forgiveness itself. Practise compassion, and you will become compassionate. Practise loving your neighbour and you will love them, even when disputes are rife. And these are just some of the steps to the deep core of the heart's secret chamber and the birth of a new heart.

Directing these aspects of desire for a holy communion with life means we utterly change within, and so our world changes without. Developing these tools means we carve out our spiritual potential, even if it is still to be fully activated in our life choices.

It isn't important that you aren't in the mood to be kind — be kind anyway - bless rather than blame the ungracious. For, to accept our spiritual potential is to accept God's love deep in the core of our being, and as our lives transform we begin to know, we begin to not just sense, but to intuit the probability of transcendence; for to transcend is to fully live the mystery of life. Then, we shine as a beacon for life, believing in all the truth that we believe in, and igniting others to do the same.

However, before we transcend we must transform our lives, particularly if they are to be as vehicles for the alchemical transcendence of flesh into spirit, and spirit into flesh. For to bring the spirit into flesh is the highest calling, wherever you may be, whatever you are doing, for the 'all' of time.

The Body And The Mysteries Of Life

Our bodies are hard-wired for the mysteries of life, and as our hearts yearn, the essential experience of intensity, intimacy and immensity remind us of whom we are, and consequently we shine with the ineffable quality of an inner glow. The glowing of our cells — the glow from within — reflects without, and the mystical path is lit.

Firstly, this pathway is begun by empowering ourselves with the knowledge that although we may be wearing the body suit of a human being that our essential nature is infinite spirit - completely liberated, suffused and full of well-being, constantly unfolding and eternal. We are light energy beings that are within an ocean of soul or pneuma, and not simply with a soul within us. This is an ancient apprehension, meaning that for thousands of years human beings have seen the force moving through the deep of the Cosmos, knowing it to be the Anima Mundi, Pneuma, Pranayama, Chi, Ki, the Force, the Holy Spirit, the Holy Wind, the Collective Unconscious or the Morphogenetic Field.

Therefore, connection to these forces is through Prayer, Meditation, and Chant (resonating with God). Then we open a current of energy that dedicates intention to our heart's voice - the seat of our soul, and our physical bodies become emblazoned with light.

Secondly, by experiencing these practices on a daily basis we create the power of stillness and peace. We are taken to a deep place within our being, which is the pure awareness of our essence. For, just underneath the surface of our normal thinking is a level of consciousness that is filled with total peace, stillness and love. To penetrate the chatter of our normal thinking, we need to move deeply into the bedrock of our inner being, and discover the 'still, small voice of God' that Elijah spoke of.

The more our lives chatter at the surface, the more we need to move to this deep space of stillness that is soul. Otherwise our lives become filled with doubt, insecurity, incoherence and disenchantment. Listen to your mind and you will tire of its discourse; silence your mind and you will connect with the Source.

Thirdly, we need to recognise that Awe and Joy are the gatekeepers of the devotional path. For without the reverence of awe in the magnificence of the divine, without the innocence of joy at the splendour of creation, what are we?

These are the concomitants that caress our hearts open, making peaceful our minds, and firing our spirits. When we move through these aspects of consciousness we literally move within the mind of God.

"The most beautiful thing we can experience is the mysterious.
It is the source of all true art and science. He to whom this emotion is
a stranger, who can no longer pause to wonder in joy and stand rapt
in awe, is as good as dead: his eyes are closed."
– *EINSTEIN*

We will now develop three of the core power tools of the heart to extend further our work in relation to the Heart's Voice.

The tools are:

GRATITUDE
NON-JUDGEMENT
FORGIVENESS

There are a number of others of course such as patience, compassion and courage, but let's begin by exploring these three core principles:

1. POWER TOOL ONE: GRATITUDE

Anyone and everyone can experience gratitude in their hearts. Yet how many of us allow gratitude to move through our daily living? Those of us that allow appreciation and gratitude to permeate our lives tend to be happier, more forgiving and most helpful to others. And so, open to a new heart by asking yourself:

- Do I thank life for the wonders of its grace every day?
- Do I govern my thoughts or words about someone with whom I experience negativity?
- Do I seek out ways of being compassionate or helpful to others every day?
- Do I attempt to transform feelings of negativity?
- Do I reward others when they speak of their triumphs in life?
- Do I grumble about not feeling well, or about being made tired by the actions of work?
- Do I see the beauty of nature every day?

Gratitude is highly magnetic. It energizes us because the vibration of gratitude is a pure conduit between the body and the soul. When we appreciate, when we feel gratitude lodged in our hearts, we automatically move from a local sense of being into the non-local awareness of our eternal being. You see, the higher vibrations of gratitude emerge from the Source.

What emerges from infinity is an unfolding possibility of creative potential, filled with harmony, and directly from the mind of God. We experience its immediate manifestation through the breath of soul, which is

God's inspirational highway; when we express gratitude we automatically link to receiving guidance from God's will, and a real sense of inner truth from our higher self.

The emotional resonance sent out by a heart full of gratitude, a heart that is full of coherent rhythm, is a magnet. The electro-magnetism of the heart produces a force that is much stronger than any other organ in your body. It sends out a charge that envelops your energy field, expanding your aura to an amazing degree. This new heart choice magnetically attracts peoples' fondness, creative opportunities, and joyous scenarios. Similarly, it produces wondrous endorphins that foster a state of physical and emotional well-being.

The world and the Cosmos expand or contract depending on our levels of appreciation, and how we breathe them. We all have known people who have very little, and yet treat life so well that they smile at a ray of sunshine, a blade of grass, or the shine of the dew on the early morning soil. When we appreciate, our revenue of abundance expands. But when we have much, and treat it badly, our coffers always appear to decrease and depreciate.

The Heart's Note – Case Study 1

A client of mine who is a successful movie actor was moving through a terrible divorce. Legal Papers had been filed by his wife, a successful TV personality, even though once they had been immeasurably happy. Michael was so in love with his wife, and yet so angry, hurt and betrayed that he appeared inconsolable.

The feelings of rejection consumed him to a point of madness, and slowly his career began to diminish - the castings became fewer and fewer, the seeming rejections more tortuous, and the hopelessness acute. We were all very concerned, awaiting revelation for the best action. For, Michael had moved out of the marital home, and his access to his two children had been denied.

Then one day a miracle occurred. Legal decisions were revoked to allow Michael access to his children, and yet he still expressed anguish about entering the once beautiful family home. As he drove up to the house, his two sons ran to meet him, and threw themselves into his arms. The look of joy, the countenance of appreciation, the ripple of gratitude on the children's faces produced such a powerful response in Michael, it reminded him of the hope that had once filled their lives together, and he wept tears of joy as he embraced his sons, a cleansing that had not occurred for many months.

The following day after the rite of meditation, he met with the casting directors of a major TV series. Within moments Michael had secured himself a part, written for him as the leading actor. A rampage of appreciation so infused his heart that it felt fit to burst, and Michael announced his bitterness had turned into better-ness.

His children's love had reminded him of the gift of appreciation, for the powerful bond he once had experienced with his wife, and the love that had brought about the creation of children. Moreover, Michael felt that the love that had been denied him was a gift in disguise, and a renewed call for him to love more fully.

We Created This Prayer To Revere Appreciation As a Sacred Vessel:

Dear God,

In truth at your shrine of creative potential, Thank you for the light you have shone on my life, Thank you for the love you have made so richly visible, Thank you for touching my heart with the hand of truth, Thank you for the sweet innocence of my children, and may it be always thus.

Thank you for the illumination of joy, Thank you for watching over me when in travail and allowing me to feel that I am not what I was, but am becoming new.

So be it.

Amen.

The Heart's Note – Case Study 2

Elizabeth was a client of mine some years ago, arriving to consult with me after her Doctors had announced that Cancer was rapidly spreading through her Lungs. Although Elizabeth had been placed on a course of Chemotherapy, her body had not responded, and her Oncologist suggested she had a maximum of six months to live.

Elizabeth felt her heart break by this news, and she was terribly distraught, feeling that the life she had once adored had dashed into horrific bleakness. I held her through this process and we began working with the merits of meditation and the sound healing processes I refer to as 'sonic showers' arising through The Alchemy Of Voice. And so, Elizabeth began to see that through a courageous shift of consciousness she might be able to identify what had created the cancer, and then heal it.

Daily prayer was crucial in the steadfast recovery of her heart's joy, and her will to live, and one day whilst she engaged in one particular prayer (see closing of this study), I remember feeling a strong Angelic presence around her that radiated powerful love. I knew in my entire being that Elizabeth would move from this oppressive landscape and fully heal her Cancer.

We created a process of detoxification. Elizabeth would work with a number of specialists: a Nutritionist, a Homeopathic Acupuncturist who specialised in Cancer, a Cranio-sacral Osteopath, a Masseur, and myself as Soul Psychologist, Seer and Sound Healer.

The initial objective was to find out what demons lurked in Elizabeth's shadow - the emotional wounds that had led to the disease: indeed, the force that had precipitated several challenging male relationships throughout her thirty-three years of life, and the bonds that had been psychologically complex and physically abusive.

Elizabeth's Father had left her mother when she was three years of age, and she grew up in an intense Roman Catholic Irish family back-ground, where guilt was used to impede transparent conversations about sex, love and power. Through the work we did on Elizabeth's second Chakra, she remembered an experience of terrible fear when her Father whom she had loved deeply, left home.

Accompanying the pain of abandonment were powerful feelings associated with the loss and the anger. All came to the fore as Elizabeth bravely uncovered section after section of unexpressed feeling states. Then, a miracle of transformation occurred.

After three months of holistic detoxification and yielding to the spiritual conviction of divine healing, Elizabeth felt a tremendous shift of force in her breast, throughout the whole of her torso.

Soon after this energy transformation, Elizabeth was booked in for a Chest X-Ray, and afterwards on receiving the result of the examina-tion, she discovered that the cancer had considerably diminished. Her joy was immense and as a consequence she felt her life was once more her own - appreciation for her body, the joy of uncovered truth, the gift of healing, the accrued blessings, all these deep feelings poured through her as she sensed her transformation from negativity into joy.

In celebration, Elizabeth decided to take a vacation in southern Ireland, where she had felt huge peace and tranquillity, several years before. Her yearning to commune with Nature and meditate further on the peace she was beginning to know as her heart's note, was considerable.

Whilst driving along a country road in Eire, she felt intuitively compelled to visit a lake indicated by her map.

Then, moving down an access road that led to the lake, Elizabeth felt she was rediscovering something very old within herself. When she eventually arrived at the Lake, she noticed the breath-taking ruins of an old House.

Elizabeth parked her car, and began to approach the Lake, when suddenly she heard a gunshot ring out from the woods on the opposite edge of the large lake. This shocked her, as the stillness of the hugely familiar place began to seep deep into the very texture of her being. She knew she had been close to this House before, but not in her present life.

A rugged man emerged from the woods carrying a double-barrelled shotgun, and a pair of dead rabbits. He approached and Elizabeth became frightened. The whole scene reminded her of emotional chaos she had experienced before, and yet she definitely knew the memory was of another time.

However, as the man approached she saw he had a kind face, and they spent a few moments talking through the lighter aspects of passing conversation: the quality of the weather, the fact that he was the Game Keeper on another estate a few miles off who had been given permission, to keep the woodland rabbits from over breeding. Apparently, the house had been derelict for many years after the tragic death of its former owner, an elderly, childless gentleman, whose family had lived in the house for over three hundred years. With this they said their goodbyes and the man strode off down the road.

All throughout this encounter Elizabeth began to make sense of the deep impressions the scene before her revealed. She knew the house intimately, and her life within it had been a long one, and that the man she had spoken to had been part of that life.

There was a vivid memory of saying farewell to a young man in uniform on the gravel drive that flanked the house. She had deeply loved him, and there was an extremely heavy sadness about the fact that he was leaving to attend military duties, which eventually terminated his life. Elizabeth believed her lover had been killed in the First World War, and that she had spent the rest of her days living in the house suffering severe heart-ache.

Suddenly the significance of this chance encounter opened vast memories from her childhood, when she had felt herself part of a very different social background from that she had been born into, and how her heart had often felt heavy with loss, resulting in constant chest and respiratory problems.

Through all of these feelings Elizabeth decided that she would open her heart Chakra further, indeed that she would open the whole of her body to profound gratitude for the life that had been restored to her.

Our last consultation proved that all Elizabeth had created in her recovery had anchored her into a substantial and exquisite belief in the healing that the power of love could bring.

This Was Our Prayer For Elizabeth's Healing:

Dear God,

In truth, I lay this problem with my life at your Altar. I yield to your Divine love and your healing. I surrender my challenges to your counsel and I open my whole body and life to your illumination.

Please show me divine healing and raise me above fear. Help me to forgive the past and see love in others as within myself.

Thank you dear God.

So be it.

Amen.

Gratitude Tasks To Illuminate The Way:

TASK ONE: Write down in your journal a challenging situation that you have recently experienced. Then write down three things about the situation that you are grateful for.

TASK TWO: Make a list of all the things you appreciate in your life. When you place these tokens in your heart's keeping, you are expanding the vessel of your heart, and developing its magnetic range through the universal law of attraction.

2. POWER TOOL TWO: NON-JUDGEMENT

We constantly seek to rise up, to transcend, and in the case of judgement, our souls desire to manifest elevation. Non-judgement is a powerful flight path for transcendence, and within this trajectory there lies a quantum-leap-potential needed for the creative evolution of the human species.

We know that no matter how mad the world can seem, when in spirit we can see such much of life as a vast illusion. For when we sit in the presence of God, we don't become more metaphysical but more simple. All we need do is to apply a few basic principles, remembering that love is at our core and gives fruit to forgiveness. We know that there is a kingdom of love to see when we truly see; which lies just beyond what meets us when we look at what is before us. The kingdom of love is what we were born to make manifest, and if we can apply ourselves wholeheartedly to the job with our whole body and soul, one day we will experience an illumined world.

However, if we judge others we separate ourselves through the power of exclusivity. Our ego oppresses us, and a deep spiritual amnesia sets in. When we judge, we forget that each of us is involved in this act of life as a communion so holy, that we co-create together daily, moment by moment, forever and for aye.

When we judge, we strengthen the stronghold of the ego, and fundamentally hurt ourselves in the process. For if we judge others we are judged in return, and every book of wisdom accounts this so. Remember, Jesus said: *"Judge not and ye shall not be judged."*

As we remember our true spiritual heritage, as we discover our Christlike sovereignty in the truth of love and compassion, we stand in the power of feeling vastly different. When we are about to judge someone, we must remember eternal innocence makes them a child of God, and overshadowed by Jesus. When we are about to be unkind, we need to remember that what we do to others we do to ourselves. When we are about to complain, we need to check ourselves with the nature of our contribution – am I about to answer through ego or listen to the voice of the heart, and so to love?

When we listen in this deep fashion, we literally become that we listen to, and so we forge a path to consciously become more of a blesser than a blamer.

The Heart's Note – Case Study 3

Several years ago I met a male client through recommendation, and who had spent three years in Prison. I didn't know the reason behind his sentence, and I was asked to provide elementary presentation skills, that would assist Adam as he made application for work. Apparently, before his sentence he had been a Financial Director within a Government Department, and I accepted the commission, assuming that Adam had been convicted for embezzlement or fraud, or some other misdemeanour in association with his role as a Financial Director.

On the appointed day Adam arrived at my private practice appearing very diffident and disempowered. He wore what looked like a second-hand suit, a very worn pair of shoes. His tall frame was stooped with depression, and his face was grey and forlorn. Altogether, he looked as though he was experiencing a very rough passage.

We exchanged pleasantries, and it became clear that Adam was fearful of any swift movement, or sudden sound, indeed anything that may appear disharmonious. His voice was extremely 'masked' speaking through clenched teeth, and completely under supported by breath. He resembled someone who had been constantly fearful of strong physical gestures, or power filled force.

Similarly, I observed that all his answers to my rather ordinary questions were monosyllabic, and lacking in vocal colour or variation. These were the simple observations I made which would begin to enable a rather more complex profile to occur, and as we began to work more deeply, I could see that Adam had experienced some minor lacerations to his lip and chin. In enquiring why, he become highly resistant, and was extremely reluctant to reveal any information, looking even more uncomfortable than before.

I determined to relax him further, to gain his confidence, and to find out what huge secret he harboured that created such tension, and as we began an introduction to breathing exercises, he began to weep, and whispered out his story through clenched teeth. Adam had been convicted for embezzlement and sexual harassment.

Surprisingly he was only thirty-eight years of age, although appearing much older. His story was bleak and horrific, and although his conviction had been associated with financial dishonesty, his fellow prisoners had been informed that he was a rapist, which meant he had been cruelly victimized in Prison. Adam had been beaten by fellow convicts, maltreated by prison officers, and on each day in prison had experienced terrible emotional insults and bodily attacks.

My heart was dismal at this account, and I felt strongly that this man required every ounce of loving support that he could be given. I felt such compassion for him in response to the horrors that he must have experienced; that whatever crime he may have perpetrated, he had certainly experienced terrible retribution from the brutally unjust situation he had spent three years living within.

Together we created an exercise regime to strengthen his breath-support muscles, to identify his signature note, and to engage in the poetic literature he so loved - for the development of tonal colour, flexibility and richness. Through a series of six sessions, Adam flourished, revealing much of his prior experience before the conviction, and I was able to mobilise him towards being interviewed and successfully employed by a financial services agency. Today, Adam is healthy, successful and married to a wonderful woman.

This Was My Prayer Of Non Judgement:

Dear God,

Please teach me forgiveness and compassion. Please take blame and judgement from this person. Please allow me to see with the eyes of grace, to hear with the ears of mercy, to feel with a body of love, and to stand on the rock of truth.

Keep Adam safe in the wings of the Angels, and allow him to be fragile and defenceless in the moments when strength is required, so that he may not be judged or judge.

So be it.

Amen.

The Heart's Note – Case Study 4

Some years ago I was invited to facilitate a workshop of 'The Alchemy Of Voice' in Massachusetts, USA. About thirty wonderful healers were called for those two days, and we worked in a wonderful building in Woods near the Ocean. I remember so well the sound of the swelling waves bringing dynamism and inspiration to our work.

All went well with the introductory process, as we began to meet through Sacred Sound and rediscover how the divine elements of earth, water, air and fire may bring us to our voice's own signature note - the song of our soul. As there were many people present who wanted to bring sound healing into their professional lives, into their intensive therapy processes, there were many questions and much lively participation.

However, there was one woman who, throughout the entire proceedings, appeared distant and aloof, and who only chose to take part occasionally. This was perplexing. She appeared to be silently cynical of the sensitive processes the work engendered, and although I attempted to communicate directly with her, she simply ignored me, looking in the opposite direction.

Since childhood I've seen Aura or energy fields, and I observed a greyish energy around her ears, throat and jaw area but this was pale alongside other powerful colours around her head. Her resolute reluctance to take part began to make me feel impatient and judging of her seeming lack of generosity. It was difficult to perceive why her apparent lack of curiosity had brought her to such celebratory and revelatory work.

Then I stumbled upon something huge; as we moved around the large room and sounded the heartfelt AH of our individual notes, I approached this participant hoping to elicit a response. In fact, I stood behind her and sent the vocal sound of a very robust AH into her, but still there was no response, and so I laid my hand over her Heart Chakra. Suddenly she turned with a jet stream of a smile emanating from her beautiful face, which moved me to tears. Like a tidal wave moving through my whole being, I realised that this person was profoundly deaf.

This experience was such a powerful teaching, such a blissful lesson to step aside from judgemental behaviour, and to observe another's behaviour impartially. Indeed, from thence onwards our journey proved to be limitless. Even more I was reminded of the power that perception has within our lives, and the tragedy of becoming non-present to the ever-creative aspect of living within the stillness of Now.

This is one of the great gifts that God has given us — the ability to perceive the world through our five senses. For through these sense portals we develop and evaluate all our attitudes and beliefs, with the power to really 'sense', and then think about the world, and its creations. This power gives us the ability to grow, to change, to be flexible about what we think and feel, and thereby we change the world. And so we evolve.

This Was My Prayer For Heartfelt Non-Judgement:

Dear God,

Please teach me innocence, so that my heart may open to the acceptance of all things created by your genius. Allow me to cleanse my misperceptions, so that my eyes truly see the beauty of your divine magic in all living beings, and throughout the whole of the natural world.

Please remove from me the strain of judgement, and make me whole to the love and tolerance of all things. Show me the way to move

aside the veils of my own ignorance, so that I may see the heaven that you have created in the life of this beauty.
  So be it.
  Amen.

Non-Judgement Tasks To Illuminate The Way:

TASK ONE: Write down in your journal the description of a situation that you have recently experienced when you judged the person or outcome. Then write down three things about the situation that are instruments of tolerance, and through which you can learn discernment.

TASK TWO: Make a list of all the things you feel judgemental about in your life. Then place the yielding of acceptance, concerning each aspect, in your heart's keeping. This will bring powerful teaching about mercy and tolerance into your heart, again developing its magnetic range.

3. POWER TOOL THREE – FORGIVENESS

Forgiveness is the most powerful sorter. Forgiveness liberates, for it takes full heart power to muster the force of this virtue. The best and only way to fuel its force is through continuous loving - not that I believe it takes prominence over the other heart tools, for they equally teach us coherence.

However, any miracle worker must be compelled to reveal forgiveness as a pure function of his or her life, and yet it is too easy for forgiveness to be easily moved aside. This occurs as we preoccupy ourselves with the myriad fixations of life, meandering through the diversions that diminish God's ability to move our lives forward in truth.

Therefore, begin to dream forgiveness placed in each rough aspect of your life. For example, in all the situations that have brought about perceived betrayal: when love was thwarted by a breaking of trust, when you felt powerfully mistreated and unfairly criticized, when you were insultingly slighted by one whom you thought loved you, when you felt your work or behaviour was being unjustly dismissed, when the gift of your heart was dashed rudely aside, when the person who had responsibility in your life behaved abusively, when someone else cruelly wronged the one whom you love, and all the other experiences. All are the taskmasters that bring us to account, whereby our love is stripped to the very skin of our being, and exposed for being truly beautiful or sorely blemished.

This is not easy, but when we are resolved by healing old wounds, forgiveness opens in the forefront of our consciousness as a talisman to unlock heaven.

Learning to become more discerning about thanking life, for each bounty, for being more patient in a traffic jam, for not springing into defence on the subway when someone is rude and non-present, for still loving one's adolescent child when he or she has been outrageous and flagrant in disrespect, for loving oneself and not being so hard on one-self - these are the simple tasks of forgiveness, relative to those that have become deeply embedded in our psyche.

For example, do you hold the scars of your physical body as a mark of spiritual endurance, as a badge of wisdom and maturity, or do you turn to the deeper issue of healing your interior world?

Self-forgiveness means firstly that woundology must be eliminated; self-forgiveness means that any behaviour smarting of the 'victim' needs to cease; self-forgiveness means that we see ourselves transparently and authentically eased of the bog of delusion, paranoia and self-recrimination; self-forgiveness means we stop blaming and criticising others, and substantiate our behaviour through insight and resolution; self-forgiveness means we stop re-acting to the pain by being defensive.

Instead, we must choose to be steadfastly moved by the shining light of love. Then, the soft balm of the deeper compassion forgiveness holds heals our wounds, and we realize that whatever the mistake or misdemeanour, it was literally the best that could be done in the circumstances.

Take a moment right now to discern if you are holding a lack of forgiveness against yourself. Being totally true with forgiveness can utterly change our lives, when we have firstly forgiven ourselves. If we hold grudges, self-blame or guilt about something in our own lives, we resist the potential free-flowing energy of the source that is the grace of God's manna feeding us.

Deep hurt takes time, patience and courage to accept fully, and to relinquish through healing. In order to plummet the depths, firstly work to soar the heights of joy, gratitude, surrender, inspiration and love. Robert Browning once said:

"Ah, but a man's reach should exceed his grasp,
or what's a heaven for."

When we reach out for help, God always hears, and we fall more gently, as we drop into the depths of the despair. God allows us to take the Angelic sensations of awe and joy, those that began the mystical pathway, and to use them as beacons of light so that we may pass through the darkness of the churning depth of emotion.

Forgiveness means that we've decided to stop letting the pain fester inside, and so a miracle is born with a new dawn shining. Thence we fully recognize that the true point of life is that we are living on Planet Earth in order to shine our light for the benefit of others, for the entire world, and that all those places where forgiveness seems blocked merely need be surrendered to God for His healing.

If we ask God He will always take the pain away, if we are ready to let it go and yield. He is always there to witness our tears, and to hold us through love in what we often perceive as the illusion of loneliness. Whatever we deny within ourselves, whatever we momentarily refuse to heal within ourselves, we unconsciously project onto others.

This makes our ability to atone and forgive so much more complicated, so much more challenging. But when we let go of these complex forms of behaviour, our spiritual muscle develops fast in the soul's gym, and so we aspire to a state of ultimate compassion. As we heal, the world heals with us. When we stand naked in forgiveness, lightness returns to our hearts and they soar, and so we know we have made it to a new place, which may just be paradise.

Through these resonances God is asking us to move beyond the domain of the local, of the literal world of physical sensing, into the non-local vastness of pure love. Then the veil of the mystery dissolves, and we see the miracle of love shining in our lives and through the lives of others.

Forgiveness, comprehended on this level, allows us to evoke the greatness of love in other people's lives, and therefore we work the miraculous. This degree of latitude means our band-width expands to absorb more light, and we become as human angels.

This powerful level of angelic forgiveness allows us to behave with mature consideration, reaching a deeper understanding about the centre of our nature, and the divinity of our soul. Therefore, we are vigilant about the deficits that once created havoc in our lives, those errors that stopped us from living the divine coherence of the heart.

The Heart's Note – Case Study 5

A client named Sebastian had held a responsible Arts' Management position for a number of years, and the organization he served was moving through a period of re-definition. New strategy was being introduced by the Board to produce optimum growth over the next three-year period.

The Managing Director was a highly gifted 'people' person, and yet couldn't agree with the foreseeable changes, and so resigned. A new Director was appointed, except this person had a reputation for being less generous, and more systems-oriented, than his predecessor.

Within a short period of time Sebastian discovered that whatever initial impressions had been gained about the new Director's organisational efficacy, his behaviour was vastly different from the former Director.

Sebastian saw his own management position being compromised. He needed to either surrender to the new regime or resign, and the latter action seemed repugnant. His love for the visionary aspect of the project was acute, and so he decided to yield to the consequences.

As time moved by the new Director found Sebastian's work, his mode of organization, even the way he presented himself, to be unacceptable. Gradually the new Director began using bullying behaviour in order to control Sebastian.

Many arguments ensued, and Sebastian felt publicly diminished by the threatening tactics of the new Director, so he decided to approach the CEO to make official complaint about the Director's behaviour. In this Sebastian felt fully seen and heard by the CEO, who ultimately pledged to arbitrate in order to make amends on his behalf with the new Director.

However, when the Director met the CEO, and was given information about his earlier meeting, the Director accused Sebastian of disloyalty, and to not accept the issues brought forth through discussion.

Sebastian felt betrayed and humiliated by both the CEO and the Director, and in despair, chose to resign. That same day as he left the office building, he tripped and fell down a flight of stone steps that led from his office; the emotional pain he experienced literally became a physical injury and Sebastian was taken to hospital. There the doctors recommended he should spend time recuperating, advising that the shoulder injury was small and would quickly heal.

That night Sebastian had a dream in which he was to be beheaded as a medieval knight. As the executioner's word lifted to strike off his head, Sebastian saw that this man bore a resemblance to the new Director. Stunned by this, he realized that he hadn't paid the executioner gold for a swift death; paying the executioner was part of a medieval code of honour, whereby the executed forgave the executioner.

As this became a realization Sebastian felt the sword fall, but it missed his partially raised head, and fell into his right shoulder, the shoulder that had been injured in the accidental fall.

Waking from this nightmare, what dawned on Sebastian was that he needed to forgive the Director, and saw that his accusation and blame had contributed to the rift between them. If he could atone with forgiveness, all would be energetically healed, and with this knowledge Sebastian slept well for the first time in months.

This Was Our Prayer For Ultimate Forgiveness:

Dear God,

Oh force of ultimate and exquisite love, Please wash my fear and hatred clean. Show me the path to the sweet compassion of forgiveness. Make me strong and constant, expanding my heart to accommodate the bravery to let go and forgive.

Hold me whilst I cleanse these wounds with my tears. Caress me when the darkness closes in. Uplift me to see the light of your shining truth. Please let your love hold me true.

So be it.

Amen.

The Heart's Note – Case Study 6

One day two years ago, I received an email from an Israeli woman who lived in Jerusalem, and was planning to visit the UK, to attend a funeral.

Tragically her son had been killed in a senseless attack perpetrated by an Islamic Terrorist group currently functioning in the UK, and she had been asked to make an address at his funeral.

Shoshanah had been recommended to meet me by non-orthodox Jewish clients of mine who resided in London. These wonderful people spent much of their lives organizing international events in support of the Peace Movement between Palestinian and Israeli Groups. Their perspective revered World Peace as an essential tenet of life on Planet Earth, and they sought a Global Coherence Initiative.

My role was to coach her for the public address that she was giving in tribute to her son, to make additions if necessary, and to generally prepare Shoshanah for the occasion that would require bravery and courage. I was deeply moved by the account of her son's life and death, and was in service to whatever I could possibly provide this resilient woman in her time of grief.

When Shoshanah arrived I was utterly surprised to experience the presence of one wrapped in celestial bliss. Instead of being the grieving victim that I had been led to believe, I met a beautiful, brave and emotionally intelligent woman, who was a moving witness of serenity.

She told me the extraordinary story of her son, and how she believed him to have been a human Angel. She said that he had given his life for the community, in order that they fully comprehend forgiveness as a visible sign of an invisible reality.

Moreover Shoshanah believed that in order for her son's soul to move forward, any aspect of grief must be released into the sanctity of his spiritual existence, that death did not exist, and that the energy be given to the compassionate work of the community. She believed that dedicating her grieving through good work for the living provided her son with the force to ascend into the consciousness of his spirit.

Shoshanah wished to uplift our minds through forgiveness, to expiate the horror and drama of terrorism, by placing all in divine grace. She believed that there were casualties on both sides of the incident, not just her son, and that forgiveness would be the balm by which we could all heal, and therefore we would go on to experience the joy and ecstasy of life once more.

There was little that I could provide for her, other than a reminder that all she needed was the support of speaking from her heart. She shared with me so generously, and added that she had been through the 'long dark night of the soul'.

She knew her son's life was in peril through information received in a dream. She knew the point at which he perished as his spirit had come to her and she had moved with him into a space of heavenly energy. It was in this space that she had received further revelation of her son's true essence.

On return to her physical body she experienced huge personal grieving. As a Mother she wept immeasurably, healing and washing her wounds. It was at this point that she felt another being enter her space. She felt her son with her surrounded by Angels, and it was at this point that she decided she must hold compassion in her heart for those who had committed the outrageous murder, to forgive their violence, and so dedicate her life to world peace.

This Was Our Prayer For The Acceptance Of Forgiveness:

Dear God,
Please show us the path to Forgiveness.
Please open our hearts to the power of Atonement.
Please give us the strength that is needed for this commitment.
Please fill us with the balm of your love.
Please show us how to liberate our hearts to acceptance.
Please ask your Angels to hold us in their grace.
Please carry us in the conviction of your love.
So be it.
Amen.

Forgiveness Tasks To Illuminate The Way:

TASK ONE: Write down in your journal the description of a situation you have recently experienced, when you were required to forgive an individual or a group of people. Then write down three things about the situation that were the instruments of forgiveness, through which you could fully embody this quality of grace.

TASK TWO: Make a list of all the things you feel unforgiving about. Then place the acceptance of forgiveness concerning each aspect into your heart's keeping. This will bring powerful teaching about love and forgiveness through your heart, expanding the vessel of your heart as a power for change, and enhancing its magnetic range.

In Conclusion…

As we can ward ourselves against the conspiracy of harm, and develop the spiritual muscle of the heart through kindness and compassion, its physiology expands and oscillates in coherence with the purity and elixir of love itself. If we can pledge ourselves to a daily ritual, to daily practice, to the development of conscious awareness, paradise occurs in our lives, and each life choice becomes a stairway to heaven. And I sincerely hope that gratitude, non-judgement and forgiveness are the power tools that bring you to your own experience of paradise.

CHAPTER FOUR

The Heart Sacraments

*An open heart is the ultimate sacrament. This is when we truly
know God as a super position for all spirit, from all things.*
~ *MATTHEW FOX*

In this accelerating and complex world there is a huge and rising hunger, on the part of just about everyone, for an authentic experience as a reconnection to what is deepest and best in us. Authenticity is made alive within us by the challenging experiences of our lives which signpost where love, kindness, patience and unity lie.

My personal lamentation is that we tend to choose grim circumstances as an anvil on which to sharpen the virtue of our authenticity; we choose desperation over inspiration. This is clear to see when we visit the world media broadcasts, which indicate the intensifying predicament of our world economic crisis. Counter intuitively, the Religious establishment protests vociferously against centralized Government, suggesting the present economic crisis is instead a severe moral crisis.

Our prayers for world peace, our desire for unity, our efforts to create peace within, are quintessential. For if we wish to change the way life looks outside, we need to first change what's happening on the inside. Carl Jung once said:

*"One doesn't become enlightened by just imagining figures of light
but rather by making the darkness conscious."*

The staggeringly grim events we see presented on our media screens of the vastly changing world of 2010 predetermine how far we may utilize the light-filled central axioms of our existence. Many use the light to bring forth the shadow and to heal it. For it is the substance of peace, and not the behaviour of war, that will ultimately heal our fear. Therefore, acts of love, faith, joy, humility, compassion, patience and gratitude, to name just a few, need to become the awakened gestures of our daily existence, to create world healing, through manifesting personal catharsis.

Meeting a Green Man

The healing of life itself can be an extraordinary journey, and often signposted by meeting a 'green' man or woman. These folk are 'gatekeepers' to the rich essence of life, and mostly appear unexpectedly, yet always when we most need them. Their teaching and their wisdom shine like exquisite sacramental jewels, yet their material lives can often be humble. One such being I met was Benjamin.

Benjamin was the senior security officer at a major establishment I often visited in order to teach. Benjamin was well known at the Centre and in the local community. All people, young and old, senior and junior, permanent staff or visitor, liked and respected him. What was it that they all saw? What was it within this man that constantly won our hearts? What sustained this radiant individual?

Benjamin was alive with the light of gratitude, the joy of life, and the gift of faith. One could see his whole being filled with an appreciation for being alive, and vitally part of everyone's existence. He literally glided through life in a state of ecstasy sustained by his humble joy.

This choice expressed itself in every cell of his being, and when people greeted him, his smile shone like the spring sun, and the rays of his love were directed to anyone who was challenged. The care he took in his appearance, the patience he illustrated with challenging members of the public, or the laughter that rang out when subtle complaints were made about the complexities of the world-all seemed at ease and in flow with Benjamin's existence.

Even if he experienced discomfort himself - he had a repetitive injury sustained in his lower back - the lure of his youthful spirit would always bring a smile to his face and a gurgle of fun from his throat.

One afternoon I remember feeling slightly disappointed in some challenging students who were ungracious about the experience they were receiving. Benjamin caught my attention, and reading my slightly disconsolate face, asked what was wrong. After my explanation he said, *"They just don't know how to hear the hush of heaven when you speak of the wonder in your heart. Just forgive, they won't forget!"*

I was speechless at the words the *'hush of heaven'*. This wonderful, simple man was an Angel from the celestial realms, on loan to us for our healing, and his benign amusement. What an enlightened soul, what a gracious spirit, what love. The level of gratitude, of peace, of joy that he radiated into the world was more valuable by far than any rich gain of material success.

He had opened his heart to the cultivation of love in the world, bestowing this energy *'like manna from heaven'* on all he met, whether they were glad or sorrowful. All the people in the locale responded in like measure.

That very night Benjamin was no more; he passed peacefully whilst sleeping next to his wife of fifty years. This man's life was a testament, and his intention was focused coherence. He was hard-wired to connect with the verities of life in essence, rather than through suffering. His joy was mined from deep within his soul, his wisdom was shaped on the anvil of experience, and his faith was made glorious by the incredulity he was in no pains to suffer.

This gentle man of no specific education was one of the learned guides that pass us as 'pilgrim souls', before they move on through the sands of time existing in a presence that is ancient. I remember he once showed me a small piece of paper taken from an old magazine, which he had kept in his wallet. On it was written:

> *"First they ignore you, then they laugh at you,*
> *then they fight you, then you win."*
> – *MAHATMA GANDHI*

When he first showed me this powerful maxim, he chuckled saying, *"And look what happened to him!"*

I loved this irreverence in him, his ability to laugh naughtily in a profound moment, just to remind us not to become sentimental, and to keep all things within flow.

Ironically, we sometimes react irresponsibly or crudely to the virtues of such a story as this one about Benjamin. We say: *"Oh that's nice,"* or *"I don't have time to talk to everyone like that,"* or *"Well that's alright for him, but not for me,"* or *"People can be very soft when they don't have responsibilities."*

In these instances I hear Benjamin saying: *"This is simply because we are unused to feeling our heart in action."*

His catch phrase was always:

"Its simple. Let go and let God!"

This was a man of no specific religion, of no time or place, of no culture, but illumined by the proportion of his own gargantuan faith.

A Test Of Faith

How can we apply these same principles when in the storm of a financial crisis, when suffering a ravaging health problem, when fractured by a warring neighbour, when made forlorn by an embittered divorce, or when made insecure by unemployment?

We must consciously and coherently use a technique that inspires us to become greater men and women. If we can become transmitters of universal healing, informed by each healed wound, formed by every scar, we are beginning to live the victory that is signified in the holy notion of the Crucifixion and the Resurrection.

In the depths of the darkness of your soul, when you are fighting with the demon of anger or hatred or shame, when all succour seems a far and distant oasis, have you ever felt that the feeling was bigger than you? You know you are right, for when we are pushed to the depth of our limits of despair, when we are moved to the height of suffering and pain, there we attune with 'collective suffering'. This vale of tears is an archetypal well of remembrance, a place where the demons of corruption lie.

This is why it is our destiny to heal ourselves with courage, mercy, refinement and grace. For when we do heal, our brothers and sisters heal too. When we experience truth, inspiration and sincerity, we feel illumination seeping through the very marrow of our bones. Therefore, our soul tingles, our heart resounds and all 'heart stabs' are cleansed. This is a preferable state to any sorrow, or any imprisonment of consciousness, or any long held torture of the soul. We're really not so separate from this peace. We just think we are.

Developing Faith

Jesus said: *"Blessed are the peacemakers for they shall be called the children of God."* To become fully alive in the sacrament of the heart, in the essence of life, we need to develop Faith, the bedrock on which love is found. It's easy to see a way of passing on heart-filled love, when we are in a situation where love is proffered.

The point is how can this connection be maintained when we experience the pains, slights and attacks from those around us who wish to project the shadow? The answer is Faith.

Faith is the substance of things hoped for, in evidence not yet seen. It is the very inner fabric of the Soul, for Faith has the inherent means to help us surrender to Divine will.

Interestingly, in our past history Faith was held in blindness. Then as we engage in the current paradigm shift, its will and force became truly visionary. For its energy in our lives sustains trust as a transcendent reality, as a rainbow lit bridge that lifts us from hell into heaven.

Our visionary capabilities enable us to be clear sighted as we pass through the darkest valley of the shadow of this current era, because we see the light on the other side. You see the visionary does not look away from the shadow, but through to the light beyond.

Jesus said: *"If you have faith as small as a mustard seed, you will move mountains."* It is this precise vision that we need at this time. Not rose-tinted or closed by delusion, but transparent and open to scrutiny.

It is difficult to have faith in a world that is moving so fast. But if we see faith as the rudder that steers our ship through the times that are changing, then we move into the flow of the universe. We give ourselves permission to become the master/mistress of our destiny. We develop brave creativity and muscled spiritual expansiveness. We become the sacred knowledge that is embedded deep within our cells, and not beyond our touch.

For it is not what we 'do' with our faith that is significant, but what we are 'becoming'. It is the visionary healing that allows us to see that the being we were before is no longer, because we have literally died to our former selves. In consequence we move forward healed, refreshed, made new for the next vision, and we sense our heart is alive with a new beat, beating with the pulse of the infinite holy instant.

Job's Story

There is an excellent Bible story about a wealthy man named Job who once had great material richness, including seven sons and three daughters. The moral of this story teaches through its revelation.

Job's faith was severely tested when his material gains were taken from him. In his despair he was further tested by three friends who doubted the word of God, and who dismissed him by judging the will of God. Job's trust was almost completely thwarted, and so he berated God, suggesting that these vile circumstances were unjust.

Then appeared a young man "with wisdom beyond his years" who suggested that it is not a man's right to know the mind of God, or to criticize the choice of Divine will.

Job's response is to supplicate, recognising his own folly, and relinquishing his own will to God's. The Holy of holies then replenishes Job's material riches more marvellously than ever before, providing him with a second family, and Job lived for a hundred and forty years.

Supplicating To The Source

Often we are sorely chastened by life, not to learn how powerless we are, but to re-vision our perspective about the material aspect of our lives. By conclusion and by pure dint of purpose, we are moved back into the essence of the heart's sacrament and the nature of spirit.

Thus, moving forward and manifesting our creative potential, not through the direction of self will, but of God's, we muster our flow in the Source by adhering to certain principles. The greatest act of faith is to supplicate our purpose to the trust of these principles, and as we bask in spirit, we glow with possibility:

Heart Stirrings To Uplift The Work Of The Heart Sacraments

1. To live in the belief of the creative flowing spirit of the Cosmos.
2. To venerate the life of the Cosmos as co-creative.
3. To create the courage to make choices and to accept uncertainty, so developing discernment.
4. To not judge and trust the unravelling events of our lives in the peace of the holy instant.
5. To bring no harm to any living energy and to honour the condition of all life with love and compassion.
6. To extol the virtues of Humankind for the knowledge and upliftment of all.
7. To develop wisdom and stillness in every action as an initiation into the 'now' of creation.

The Heart Sacraments Meditation

- Move to your Sacred Space, and please make sure you are not disturbed.
- Light a candle, play healing music, burn some incense: all to create an ambience for receiving specific guidance with regard to the sacraments that arise from the secret chamber of your heart, the peaceful kingdom which is the very seat of your soul.

- Make sure you have paper and pencil, or your journal, just in case you wish to write notes.
- If you are used to meditation and wish to sit cross-legged on the floor, then please follow that intention. Otherwise, find a comfortable chair to sit on, and earth your body with your feet on the floor.
- Loosen tight clothing and please sit with your spine aligned, removing any covering from your head. Try not to use the back of the chair, as leaning against the back of a chair can compromise your breath by collapsing or bending your spine.
- Make sure your feet are on the floor with shoes off, and place your hands comfortably on your lap in the shape of a Mudra.
- Feel your spine reflecting the, I AM THAT I AM presence in its aligned status. Visualize the Pranic Cord as a laser beam of light shining through the whole of your spine. Make this a colour of your own choosing, or visualize gold as an Angelic vibration connecting your heart chakra as a passageway between body and mind.
- Visualize the Pranic cord moving down through your spine and the levels of the floor beneath you, through to the ground floor, the basement, the earth's surface, the soil, clay, stone and rock, anchor finally into bedrock. See the cord anchor into Mother Earth, and notice how magnetic gravity draws you into the very womb of the Divine Mother. The Gaia is always present, holding us in unconditional love through gravity. It's just that we often forget her embrace through the fixation with 'doing'. Whereas Divine Mother always encourages us to let go, to yield, to flow with the currents and cycles of life, and not to resist.
- Pause for a moment or two in anchoring, and then journey up through the cord again, siphoning the flow of Divine Mother's energy up through the successive levels of rock, stone, clay and soil - reversing the process you took earlier.
- Visualize the Pranic Cord moving upwards through the building, through the whole of your spine, into the upper spine, and then through the upper floors of the building in which you are placed. See the cord moving further into Father Heaven's Universe, and off into your Cosmic planetary home. If you are unaware of this, simply see the cord travel to the Planet Venus, the Goddess of love. Venus is the brightest star in the night's sky and particularly opens the vibration of this heart centred work.
- Move to your Heart Chakra and rest for a moment. See the power of this central organ emanating through the whole of your body, like

a six-pointed star emanating into the Cosmos. If you can visualise a halo surrounding the star, you will refine its power and protect its magic ~ the six-pointed star signifies the meeting between the above, and the below: in this case the union of earth and heaven, of Mother and Father.

- As you visualize the Star over your heart, before you and behind, see it about seven inches (17cm.) in diameter and then let the breath leave your body. Wait in silence. Then when you feel ready to receive breath, breathe in as though it were light through your nostrils, and down into the whole of your being. Let it journey down your spine, like an elevator moving down a shaft, and then sound the OM three times, on three flowing breaths.

- Move the sound of the OM through the centre of your heart star. This activates the powerful forces that linger in the secret chamber of your heart. Like whispers of heaven, they will flow as exquisite Sylphs throughout the whole of your being. Visualize these eternal energies moving with gentleness through the entirety of your physique. Then wait a moment and rest.

- Check the responses of your body. You will probably feel your senses extremely heightened. Perhaps you will experience an out-of-body feeling. Fully sense that you are supported by the spirit of the ancient ones, and so remain grounded and firmly rooted to your physical frame.

- Then, when you are ready, sound the OM a further four times ~ this will total seven in all. We are using the OM as a Cosmic Key to the secret chamber of your heart.

- Pause in stillness, observe how your body feels or responds, and you will notice how the whole of you soaks in the 'space of soul', a vast space that reaches throughout infinity. Notice how you are shaped in the reality of the moment by the Axis & Anima Mundi principles, moving vertically and horizontally through your body. These vectors contain your body within its Merkabah, and thence within the energy field of infinity.

- Reach into the secret chamber of your heart. Visualize the chamber as an ambient sacred space that resonates with your highest intention.

- Visualize the sacred chamber as an exquisite Golden Temple where beautiful music plays and incense leaves the air fragrant. Fill it with wondrous fabrics and seven exquisite marble altars.

- On each of the seven altars, you will see a large Golden Crucible filled with holy water. The water has been blessed in each chalice by the Archangels.

- These crucibles are Scrying Pools, and the seven marble altars are dedicated to each of the seven Sacraments. They are a visible sign of an invisible reality that emanates as a holy intention. They are rich symbols with future promise, for you to become what you desire, and to help you on your path as you reveal the way your Heart Speaks.

- As you move through the Secret Chamber looking into each Crucible one at a time, sound each of the seven Chakra Sounds we used before. Dedicate one sound to each Crucible. The sounds act as a talisman to stir the magic of the holy water, and you will see the sacrament appear as letters on the Altar.

- They are, from the Base to the Crown:

HAW	–	IMMERSION
HOO	–	INITIATION
HOH	–	COMMUNION
HAA	–	INVOCATION
HAY	–	PURIFICATION
HI	–	ORDINATION
HEE	–	DEDICATION

Record what intuitions you receive in your journal. Then pause. Listen to the silence and say a prayer in reverence of this space:

Dear Heart,
Thank you for revealing these wondrous Sacraments.
Thank you for knowing that my intention is to be pure.
Please teach me the purpose of what I have seen.
Please illuminate the conviction of that I evoke.
I see you, dear heart clothed in supernal light.
I feel you providing ultimate well being as life and love occur.
My love is yours.
So be it.
Amen.

Slowly, withdraw yourself from your Heart's secret chamber closing down the rotations of the Heart Chakra, and allowing the six-pointed star to dematerialize into your body. Draw in your Pranic Cord, and see both the vertical Axis Mundi and the horizontal Anima Mundi drawn back into your physicality. Feel yourself soaking in stillness, with the alpha and omega of your breath suspended in space, as this rhythm gives us a sense of the true continuum in the creativity of life itself.

Imagine that the whole of your energy field is covered by a veil of golden light. This will insulate, protect and shield your force. Then be still and receive the ministrations of Love from the Cosmos.

Sense yourself to be soaking in the holy instant, where nothing matters other than what we 'be'. When we rest in this sacred moment, we rest in the Source, remembering that in fact we never left.

What you have recorded concerning the Sacraments from the Secret Chamber of your heart will resonate with you for some time, and so please continue to soak in the stillness, processing all that has happened through the entirety of your consciousness. Give all time to expand and be processed. *All Is Well.*

The Seven Heart Sacraments

The seven sacraments lie at the core of our spiritual power. They emanate from the rings of light within the field of energy known as the Source. They are made manifest in our physical lives by embodying the principles of their creation. They wait for us to activate them, in the knowledge that we are divine beings in human form.

Each sacrament is a symbolic rite representing a stage of empowerment that invites Divine Grace directly into the body of our life. When open, the force of this energy moves through our physical, emotional, mental and spiritual bodies in a similar way to the transformative energies of the Buddhic Chakras and Christian Sacraments.

The Chakras are the databases, the bio-computers for the whole of our circuitry, and the Sacraments direct us to harness our life force from the very core of our being through certain rituals or rites of passage, and gently deposit us in our heart. Therefore, they finely balance our body, soul and mind, for they are rich with purpose.

As these sacraments are divine in origin, receiving them allows us to fully comprehend that we are reflections of Divine power. When we become fully aware of their part in our lives, we feel the caress of the Divine upon us, we hear the 'still small voice of calm', and we see the miraculous revealing love in each moment of the day.

Co-Creating The Universe

The sacraments give us an understanding of how to co-create life within the Universe, because they function through communion. They lead us to how we may advantage life as we re-create ourselves in the image of the Divine. For we have always wished to merge our bodies with the Divine, by uplifting the highest quality of our character. In the sacred we find a higher vibration of consciousness, where the 'word' is truly made flesh within us, because it emanates from God.

Striving for this countenance through often testing circumstances, we are allowed to vision our lives full of spiritual sovereignty. We see ourselves ordained with a maturity that enables a supernal refinement to take place, where the only option is love. Then if we can allow our lives to feel caressed with compassion, we acknowledge that growth is an evolutionary venture and that each moment matters - this teaching creates a continuous unfolding of truth, and the sacred contract we made before incarnation begins its fuller unfolding.

SACRAMENT ONE: IMMERSION

To be *Immersed* in heart, to be deluged by the soul of the Divine is a possibility that calls to us in each breath. For within each breath exists both the alpha and the omega, the beginning and ending of our life. More so, within the great ocean of breath we are awakened by symbolic baptism, for we are immersed in the acknowledgement of our membership to 'humankind', and our interconnectivity within creation. For every breath, every thought, every feeling, every action has a vibration which affects the living field of the Cosmos that we are part of.

Energy and information at the purest level are always soaked in truth, and so this is the passageway between human judgement and divine reasoning. To glean from the fire of each day's Sun, to be drenched in the holy wind which brings hope to mind, to wash in the ocean of Soul, to feel the rock of stability beneath one - these are the elements that bring us to revere and thank the notes of each heart sacrament, for in gratitude, we are bestowed by a gift of grace. In this spark of light All Is One.

Tribal Identity

From a literal point of view, the sacrament of *Immersion* sees us conjoined with our tribal identity, and with the branches of the tree of life that determines the personal power of the Me. All the qualities that most matter to us grow from the branches of these interactions; they are the qualities associated with social ease, honour, loyalty, moral rightness and ethical conduct.

From a symbolic point of view, to be fully *Immersed* in this sacrament is to honour one's ancestors, one's family and the broader community of humanity, for this is the larger part of who we are.

The Heart's Note - Case Study 7

I met a forlorn John at a three-day workshop in Dublin, Eire. John was fifty-five years of age and single. Like most Irish men of his generation he had been reared in the tradition of Roman Catholicism, had been educated by Fathers from the Society of Jesus, and yet had moved away from organized Religious dogma in later years. However, during our work together I discovered that John had been sexually abused by a priest teacher whilst at school, and had never felt at one with the tribal nature of city life.

John's family, once large, had over the years dispersed; his parents were long dead, and apart from one estranged brother who was living in America, his other siblings had died through alcoholism, cancer, a stroke and three in a fatal road accident.

As a young man he had fallen in love with a beautiful young Irish woman and a child had been born, but they had never married. His lover received terrible retribution, was shunned and called a whore by her community. In shame John had never met his daughter. However, just before our meeting he had learned that she lived in London.

John lived alone in County Kilkenny, and felt a profound attachment to the countryside, the very soil and folklore of Ireland. Although a talented artist, he worked as a mechanic, specializing in the repair of motorcycles. John was a recluse, hardly ever spoke and experienced tumultuous depression ~ he was disenfranchised from society, and felt so isolated he contemplated suicide.

During the workshop John told his story, telling us that one day, as he thrashed around in the depths of his horror, he had switched on the Radio. The Radio was tuned to the BBC Home Service and he listened to an interview with me about the nature and essence of my voice work. The following day he purchased *The Alchemy Of Voice*, and suggested that this chance encounter and the information I gave completely changed his life, because it gave him hope. His appearance at the workshop was as a consequence of this action.

John's heart was crying out to speak its own magic, and yet he had no reason to know what it was, he was so removed from his tribe. During the workshop John received an *Immersion* in pranayama and sound, so we reconnected him physically with the ocean of soul.

Having experienced this sacrament, we turned to the literal organization of his choices, those that would provide information about how he could heal the demons of the past and then practically reconnect with the community, which gave John the strength to move back into town life. Finally, he has reconnected with his daughter in London, is courageously developing his artwork, and has met someone he knew from his childhood whom he feels passionate about.

SACRAMENT TWO: INITIATION

The second sacrament is concerned with the essence of *Initiation*. Its core nature stirs us to honour our heart, and to take the first step to truly acknowledge the presence of the *I AM THAT I AM* energy within our lives.

Above the lintel of each Temple door in the ancient world was written: *To Thine Own Self Be True*. As each person entered, they moved through a highly sensitive personal bio-identity check.

Before proceeding into the holy of holies, each individual was required to score the map of truth, by examining at first the level of integrity within self. This action of personal honouring, shaped in the prism of the moment, creates such a clear intention, for it is only with the knowledge of the 'truth within self' that one can enter into the reverence of the miraculous. The pre-requisite is the courage to open one's heart.

The lodestone of this lintel reminds us of the creation of that part of the human being that is infinite, and therefore aligned with that which is most sacred. And, as we are initiated, as we personally initiate the 'conscious self', we experience the flow of power between us and other people.

The bond we form with ourselves is the most crucial spiritual challenge that we may face. Its essence lies in a profound rite of passage, when we shift from an external reliance of power to an internal gravity, and so we truly become alive inside.

This brings with it the acceptance of our notion of 'tribal recognition', because in a flash of insight we solve a problem that had hitherto been an overwhelming feat. This growth of personal power can be an arduous task, and yet once we arrive it feels that we've approached the very gate of heaven.

The Heart's Note - Case Study 8:

During a New York workshop conversation a few years ago, I was introduced to the life of Barbara.

As a child Barbara had shown intellectual brilliance far surpassing her parents' expectations. Barbara's father was a leading City Attorney, who had inherited considerable wealth from an industrialist father, and both Mother and Father were pillars of the community, regularly donating large sums of their personal fortune to artistic and charitable foundations.

During the early stages of Barbara's education she was hailed as a Savant, with a propensity for languages, and by the time she reached her thirteenth year, Barbara was fluent in seven languages.

Barbara was the only child of her doting parents, and was unconsciously described by them as the scion of the family, a role usually taken by the eldest born male.

At the age of thirty Barbara was still living with her parents, and had been unemployed for some considerable time, even though she had gained a superb degree from Harvard. Barbara's academic intelligence had been tested through the Mensa process, through which she achieved high percentages.

During our first one-to-one consultation Barbara appeared terrified, and I was touched by the brilliance of her eyes, for they yearned for love even if she also appeared profoundly introverted. It was then I intuited Barbara had Cervical Cancer.

I learned that Barbara had fallen in love with a female fellow student at Harvard, who was also an extremely gifted linguist. Barbara was convinced that her sexuality was lesbian, having been strongly sexually attracted to women for as long as she could remember, and she was terrified that her parents would discover this.

Apparently, there had been a distant member of the family who had been ostracised, as she had lived an overt lesbian lifestyle. In consequence, the whole family had recoiled in horror, and Barbara was terrified that the same thing would happen to her.

We developed a strategy enabling Barbara to see a way of revealing her truth. The first aspect of the work was to gain acceptance of her self-love, the love of her body's sensuality. This meant initiating powerful healings to release the myriad blandishments that had led to the personal denial and fear that had in turn brought her to Cancer.

Through medical supervision, massage, body revitalising techniques, nutrition, reflexology, acupuncture, sound healing and soul psychology, we were determined to achieve a radical cure. Barbara agreed to the entire schedule of healing, recognizing that this was to be her own rite of passage, her time to finally open her heart to love, and to initiate herself into honouring who she was.

Barbara was provided with a vital, compassionate support system over a period of six months, and eventually when we met for our final session, the person that met me was a completely changed being. Empowered, healed (in remission from Cancer) and vitally reformed.

Having moved from her parent's apartment a month prior to our final meeting, Barbara was meeting them that day to announce that she was a Lesbian. We celebrated the *joy* of this huge transition, and Barbara reported that she felt fully prepared for absolutely any reaction from them.

Barbara had taken herself through a powerful process of constant positive visualization, which we believed had also brought her to a profound position of healing. Consequently, her self-loathing had been transformed into the beauty of expressive love.

Rites of Passage, in the form of profound *Initiation* can often take the form of a pilgrimage, where we journey to the mystical light of a holy shrine. However, our pilgrimages are often internalized and take us deep into the shadow, in order to heal the demons of the underworld, and so that we breathe the light of transcendence. Barbara's journey had been one such pilgrimage, brought about by the conviction of her own honouring of self.

SACRAMENT THREE: COMMUNION

The sacrament of *Communion* radiates from our heart's secret chamber as a direct line from the Divine matrix. It acknowledges everyone we know as significant, as being part of our life's design. It exists to sanctify whom we wish to "break bread with," and its theme is a deep appreciation for the essence of the broader spiritual community as a vessel through which love can be expressed.

The quality of this communion establishes a covenant force, which exudes a field of light – a circle of force that is the inclusivity of the Divine Feminine. Its power teaches us to clearly see our lives as cyclic creations, placed within the cycles of the years, the planet, the universe and the cosmic world of nature.

The Heart's Note - Case Study 9:

A few years ago in Dubai I met Caspar and Judy, who told me their extraordinary story of *Communion*.

They had first met at University in Scotland during the early sixties, and had fallen deeply in love at their initial meeting. At that time there were strict campus rules about co-habitation between members of the opposite sex, and so these two loving people decided that exploring the sexual side of their relationship was inappropriate. You see, they were coming of age during an era when innocence was maintained by its own purity, as well as by stringent social mores, and so theirs was a very different attitude from the students of today.

Caspar and Judy planned that as soon as graduation occurred, their marriage would take place and family planning would begin. However, unknown to Caspar, Judy had experienced a near fatal riding accident during her sixteenth year, and as a result had experienced a traumatic hysterectomy. Judy was terrified of telling Caspar for fear that he wouldn't marry her. Having suffered such a severe injury during mid-puberty, Judy had carried herself through many debilitating symptoms, which meant that the subject of her sexuality was extremely sensitive.

This trauma had been intensified by the fact that her dear Mother had been killed in a car accident a year after her riding incident. There had been little feminine support for her during the recovery, and she was deeply worried that Caspar would reject her if she found sex a challenging activity.

Little did she know that at the same time Caspar worried about the intensity of what he felt for her, for he was fearful that he would be rejected if he showed his passion. Their desire to explore sexual communion was an intense spiritual awakening, as they felt their souls were divinely coupled, and they saw sex as a metaphor for their deep and truly heightened love.

A few weeks after their graduation they began life together by renting accommodation, and on their first night they made passionate love, during which Judy experienced a profound healing of her sexual inhibitions, caressed by the trust in Caspar's passion. Caspar described his part in this as a Kundalini awakening, and they both felt an ancient connection surging in the ecstasy of their lovemaking throughout the whole of their beings.

The following morning, as they discussed their bond with one another, Judy revealed the secret hat she couldn't conceive of a child. Caspar was so devastated by the fact that Judy hadn't trusted him with this information earlier that he dramatically declared that he never wanted to see her again. Judy was devastated and thrown into deep mourning, and even considered ending her life.

Then, a seeming miracle occurred through a chance encounter with an old school friend named Marie. Marie's brother Philip had recently graduated from Oxford, having gained an excellent Law degree. Philip's charm and urbanity led to an impressive interview technique, and he had successfully secured a teaching position at Columbia University in New York City.

Judy and Philip had dated once or twice when they were younger, particularly when their families had taken vacations together, and they had both fancied one another since that time. Philip was an extremely attractive man, and after a few meetings together, Judy decided to leave the United Kingdom and find a new life with him in the USA, where she threw herself into building a strong relationship with him.

And yet whatever he did, she couldn't bring herself to fully love him in the same way she had committed to Caspar, although Philip's deep love for her meant that she was able to explore, release and heal the remaining demons she possessed in relation to her sexuality, particularly the perceived rejection she had experienced with Caspar. Philip's loving was tireless, and yet he was unaware of the transformation in Judy, as she felt it was inappropriate to confide in him.

Little did Judy know that Caspar was engaged in a relatively similar experience, a few hundred miles away. In fact he had become engaged to Jane, a young woman he had met whilst at Oxford, the daughter of a wealthy Connecticut family. Jane had acquired a very good degree and decided to study her Masters back home at Yale. Caspar and Jane had a sumptuous wedding, after which Caspar gained employment in the family business, based not far from New Haven, Connecticut.

So you see, idyllic relationships were created as though they were mirroring each other, and yet these bonds only lasted for ten years before divorce proceedings took place. Fortunately, no children were involved. Jane, like Judy, had experienced a traumatic accident during her seventeenth year and it had been suggested that it would be catastrophic if she attempted to conceive. Both couples divorced on the same day, and in the same year.

Throughout this period of time, these two people still continued loving the mystical communion they had established all those years before. The transference of heartfelt energy was so powerful that they were psychically mirroring one another's life.

Two years later on New Year's Eve they were both invited to the same party in New York City. By this time they were individually moving through the higher echelons of US society, having spent time since their divorces developing significant spiritual practices, juxtaposed with extremely lucrative careers. Can you imagine their surprise, when they both encountered one another at that party?

They both laughingly suggested to me at our first meeting that there was a sense of tremendous relief, and at the same time a feeling of huge expectation. Before twelve o'clock had struck, they had exchanged all significant details about their former years. The degree of communion that opened between them far surpassed their earlier connection, and on this occasion was nourished by the experience of their more mature faith.

At our meeting in Dubai they had been together for thirty years, and both had highly successful healing practices in the United States, having both trained as sexual therapists specializing in trauma. The love of their communion was so radiant, so compassionate, the effect of their energy field was palpable - the celebration of their heart conscious communion emanated such joy that all people were magnetically drawn to them.

SACRAMENT FOUR: INVOCATION

The heartfelt power of this sacrament is divine love itself, called forth through ardent supplication. When invoked it emerges as a spark of infinity, an eternal pouring forth of the nurturing life force, springing from the love-light circuitry of the Source.

In human form this materializes through the expression of unconditional love and the heartfelt gifts of beauty and harmony. The fulfilment of this heart sacrament lies in the marriage between oneself and the greater Soul.

Invocation is a daily goodness. If we can engage in a ritual of praise, and thank God for getting us through, in that we have, by the grace of

God endured. Then, whatever our relationship with God, whether it be without definition or that we are in regular contact, God loves us still as the ever flowing light of the Universe. For, our purpose is to invoke each other's greatness, and to attempt working a daily miracle in each other's lives. Therefore, ask yourself: what miracle have you created from your own heart today?

The Heart's Note - Case Study 10:

Rupert was a former student of mine who had spent only a few years exploring the highly volatile life of an Actor, before developing a successful business as a Performance Coach. Rupert was an entertaining and generous character, who lit up a room whenever he entered it. As a consequence varying businesses within the corporate market engaged him fully, and Rupert's charismatic personality brought heightened states to his clients that excited, inspired and satisfied their needs.

Professional life was rich and action packed, and yet personally Rupert felt isolated, insecure, and emotional drained. The truth was that he spent his life using activity after activity after activity to move away from the core of himself. This meant that he created diversions rather than face the gnawing pain in his own heart – project after project came along to anaesthetize the desolation he truly felt inside.

Eventually, through the consultations I sensed that Rupert felt a huge and profound loss by the absence of his Mother. When Rupert's brother had died 15 years prior, he had projected all of his grief filled anger onto his Mother, and they hadn't spoken since. His projected blame was as a result of his Mother forgetting to give his brother information about severe weather conditions, before he sailed to his death, for both brothers had been keen mariners.

When we explored the way Rupert felt about his brother's death, we also discovered that his core desolation arose from the fact that he hadn't answered his brother's phone call around the time that he had perished. Evidently the call was a distress message, and Rupert had traumatically mirrored the cut off, by stifling the connection with his heart, so as not to feel the profound gaping loss of his brother.

As younger men they had spent much time celebrating what they perceived to be a love of life. They had explored the natural world, and felt complete affinity with the calm, and roughness of the ocean, trusting in the eternal force of the nature's power. Rupert commented on the fact that his heart would sing whilst sailing, that there had been a deep core resonance experienced within his body, which he hadn't occurred since the accident.

We talked through a strategy of reconnecting with the core value of *Invocation,* and he wept for the first time in 15 years. The power of 'tears' to cleanse, to release, to unburden, to heal, is astonishing.

Rupert is now in communication with his Mother, having revisited their equal trauma formed by the spectre of the unreconciled death, and their relationship is healed. He is also back sailing, working as an Endurance Coach, teaching young people core skills associated with eco-sustainability, living in harmony with nature, and feeling Earth Mother's force sustaining the breath of life.

Opening this powerful sacrament of the heart allows the richness of Divine love to pour through you. If we close off the possibility of this grace, our whole soul vibration becomes severely bound.

SACRAMENT FIVE: PURIFICATION

All the great Saints and Holy Beings, all of our great spiritual teachers offer this sacrament as the core of their teaching. For to gain mastery at this level of consciousness is to gain union with Divine Will.

This is the sacrament that symbolically offers likeness to the notion of confession in the Christian Church – when we give our lives to God we surrender our personal will to the divine. By yielding our control of life to divine flow, by relinquishing ourselves to the notion of faith in love, our heart expands, and God steps in to repair all ill.

I believe that when we surrender to Divine authority we are liberated from temporal illusions. All the negative thoughts or actions, all past fears we have engaged in, that stop us from gaining the level of integration that is our birthright, are washed from our hearts, and our hearts open like exquisite flowers. Conversely, if we remain gripped by negativity, we create toxicity that poisons our bodies, hearts and souls. Remaining unconscious to these vibrations, perpetuates a life that is devastatingly unsustainable.

The Heart's Note - Case Study 11:

Lena was Lebanese, and at the age of thirty-three had seen some of the most atrocious acts that human beings could ever witness; war through civil strife.

However, Lena's family were materially wealthy, and she had been educated in the west. Three months before our meeting she had been diagnosed with Laryngeal cancer.

When we first met she appeared highly sensitive, and with a deep inner sadness, as though her heart was yearning for an acknowledgement or absolution. Her condition was so acute she appeared to be unconsciously 'weeping'. Through every sound, through every word, through every breath there was an unexpressed sigh.

During our first session Lena looked deep into my eyes and suddenly said, "You see, don't you?" Lena was a Sensitive, and yet as a child in war-torn Beirut, whenever she dreamed about someone, they would die. Therefore, Lena had been told by her family to "stop her craziness, and shut up!" One brother had even told her that she had literally caused the death of a neighbour's child, even though the child's death had occurred through an incendiary explosion. This child had been an intimate friend of Lena's, indeed, the families were very close, and so this accusation had a devastating effect on her.

When I 'read' Lena's aura, it was as though the whole of her physique from pelvis to head was bound in hoops of steel, each one of them being a fear that had authority over her, and as I gained Lena's trust, we unfurled these hoops of steel. Many challenging, unresolved horrors had become stuck in her energy field, and had evolved into the crystallizations of negativity within her aura. She was surrounded by negative elementals.

However, Lena talked very fluidly about the horrendous substance of her unexpressed pain, and we were able to develop appropriate strategies to release the bound force. We did this gradually as the layers unbound, and consequently Lena's heart's voice opened, showing the freedom that was within her reach.

There is a belief in our contemporary world that it should take years and years of psychotherapy to heal life's painful memories. My experience is that once located, healing can be rapid; that is, if the power that created the challenge can be clearly determined. This recognition lies at the core of the sacrament of purification, and enables us to perceive the extent to which cellular healing can take place.

During one particular session, it was apparent we had reached a critical point in our work together, and suddenly Lena asked: *"Do you believe in the Angelic kingdom?"* My response was simple: *"Of course, for how could I do this work without belief in and help from Angels of Grace."* A huge sigh emerged from her body, accompanied by a loud scream, and then much laughter, after which she revealed. *"Finally I have permission to believe in the force I have always seen, and yet was told did not exist because I just imagined it all!"*

We colluded with Lena's Angels as she relaxed, yielded, and trusted her heart purification process. In so doing Lena relinquished all effort to divine will and her power grew and grew. Therefore, Lena's Seer-ship became stronger and stronger. One morning when she woke, there were three large white feathers lying on her duvet, so pure in pearl-like hue that they could have literally dropped from heaven. As Lena told me this, she laughed and laughed in joy.

The crowning glory came when we discovered that Lena's Laryngeal Cancer was in remission. The tumour had considerably shrunk and there was a 98% possibility it would completely heal. Lena was ecstatic. The horror she had once experienced had been purified, had been transmuted into a source of inspiration, and a gift of grace.

To this day Lena gives of herself to the non-local world of her Angels, knowing that these skin-suits we dwell in through the local world are mere coverings that contain our essential nature as infinite spirits.

SIXTH SACRAMENT: ORDINATION

This heart sacrament urges us to be authentically conscious in each moment, in each day, in each month, and in each year - to not attempt determining life's meaning, but to truly discern its quality.

Therefore, each aspect of our truth-seeking beseeches us to awaken to our spirit, to consciously seek *only* the truth, to radiate *only* love, so that we may truly become vessels for the divine, and reflect only the sacred in each gesture and action.

The embodiment of *Ordination* draws awakened consciousness through each portion of our loving; our love for self as a gift to others becomes the only truth. This can happen within our immediate locale, with our family or friends, in the broader community of our neighbours and colleagues, our planetary fellow beings, and beyond to the non-local spiritual force of multi-dimensional consciousness.

There is a time in our lives when we are ordained in the ministry of resurrection, and truly see the miracle of love healing all of our lives. In becoming conscious of this devotion we develop the ability to detach from subjective observation, and we see truth as a miraculous invention, because we see it from a metaphoric perspective.

Detachment doesn't mean that we cease to care, but rather that we develop a spiritual authority that doesn't react to the voice of fear which much of life can be hostage to. When personal power reaches this degree of resolution, when we receive awareness from our hearts because they are anointed, true sovereignty begins to emerge charged with wisdom and mercy – all choices made are the same as the divine choice.

For example, it is said of Barack Obama as an 'ordained leader', that when he disagrees, he is not disagreeable, that when he speaks he is moved by a moral compass, that when he seeks compromise, he holds onto principles that can never be compromised, and that he assumes the best in everyone, instead of the worst. This man thinks 'out of the box', sees whole systems by multi-tasking, is empathetic and non-judgemental, and is proactive with opportunities that arrive in each moment. These are some of the characteristics of the 'anointed one' ordained for public service as a visionary leader.

The Heart's Note - Case Study 12:

Anita was an impressive Business Woman who sought out my private practice to improve her presentation style. Anita was an experienced, artful communicator, always focused, concise and economic in delivery, and yet she lacked warmth of tone, passion, and empathy in her voice. Anita wanted to acquire a magnetic delivery, to appear with more presence, and to express all with true charisma.

Ultimately charisma means 'charity'. It is created by unconditional love bestowing sacred healing, and in ancient times the graces of the *Charisma* were seven in number. They were believed to be directly inspired by the Holy Spirit, and were given by God as a gift for transformation.

As a senior HR Director within a major pan-global company and holding a high calibre business portfolio, Anita had received requests to speak at major business conventions, to give keynote presentations on themes such as: "Emotional Intelligence for Senior Management" and "Intuition in the Workplace." Both were future-facing subjects, and not common currency in the Corporate Market at that time of her life's witness.

Anita was pre-ordained by her sheer grace and serenity, she exuded compassion and mercy, and during our early meetings it was apparent that she had little awareness of the considerable impact she could have on the community at large. I saw it as my task to encourage her into the acceptance of her role as an ordained consciousness. I broached the subject gently during our second consultation, and Anita confessed that she had a recurring dream where her position as a spirited leader was constantly evoked.

In her dream, she was always female, and yet seemed to move between two incarnations; firstly as an emancipating politician and secondly as a pioneering pilot, who flew solo. When I emphasised the symbolic nature of each role, Anita laughed. It had never occurred to her that the dream was prophetic.

Not that she wasn't creative, not that she didn't engage with the metaphor of life, but more because she was flabbergasted by the close proximity of the two passions she had day-dreamed of since her teens. These passions had never reached fruition, for one was a fierce sense of injustice, and the other an absolute love for heights.

Anita's performance style evoked the stamina of the archetypal warrior and as the archetypes are keys into our consciousness, I decided to elicit their strengths. In the pantheon of the ancient Greek Goddesses, Anita's quality can be best illustrated by the character and behaviour of the robust Pallas Athena, the Goddess of War and Wisdom.

For Anita was far too invasive for many audiences, and we needed to balance the fervour of her liberationist tendencies with the archetypal lover, as seen in Aphrodite, the Goddess of Love. Anita agreed that in balancing these energies her process would appear more harmonious, and more magnetic, so we set about creating a strategy.

During these consultations my admiration for Anita grew and grew, as she achieved the delivery we had defined. Through seemingly effortless ease, her new stance meant that she could negotiate board members and key audiences into a greater tolerance for ethical and inspirational behaviour; this would undoubtedly encourage altruistic objectives into the commercial market.

Through experience Anita truly began to live the finer aspects of her spiritual consciousness, accepting the notion of Ordination as a sacrament of the heart, and then by completing her training as a licentiate Pilot.

SEVENTH SACRAMENT: DEDICATION

The sacrament of *Dedication* marks a point of completion, arising from the disciplined experience and acquired wisdom of the former sacraments. It is a gateway to transcendence through a fuller apprehension of being at one with the great heart of the Universe.

When we move through this gateway, a higher vibration of love is experienced. It is then that we are made aware of a sensation that is elevated beyond the immediate proximity of what we have perceived as possible. For it is here that we step into a kingdom where love is the only thing, and this is the love that passes all understanding. In this we are in tune with the holy instant, drawing the divine into our flesh, deep into our very bones.

Before passing through this gate, we are asked to call our spirit back from any unresolved experience. This can be a painful time when our mortal flesh is challenged. In this we must search life through thought-filled silence, and truly perceive where our spirits have become fixed.

Spiritual life means naming the pain, surrendering it to God, and asking for it to be cleansed by the Angels - this dedicated scrutiny is often called 'the long dark night of the soul'.

When we transmute the pain, when we truly surrender emotions such as guilt, rage, jealousy, fear, hatred, abandonment or regret, we pass through this sacred gateway to a place of renunciation. We dedicate our lives to reveal the innate spirit of its essence, by learning to truly embody love. It is then that wisdom floods our lives and service becomes a reality.

The Heart's Note - Case Study 13:

Pierre had been a Dominican Friar for 15 years, and was recommended to me by a Healer of Transpersonal Psychology, who had experienced a similar challenge on the pathway to *Dedication*. When Pierre came to see me, he was profoundly enveloped in 'the long dark night of the soul', and contemplated suicide.

Pierre felt that all connection with the Divine had left, and was living in a state of utter dread, whereas before he had experienced a consistent state of grace in communion with the Divine. What intensified this despair was a feeling of 'spiritual madness' in the loss of his identity; he described this as a form of 'ritualized schizophrenia'.

Through the faith that had sustained his spiritual practice for so many years, he believed his current pain was based on an unexplored schism between his physical and emotional body. For as long as Pierre could remember he had been sexually attracted to men.

Pierre had been brought up in rural France by very loving and devoted parents. Family life had been simple, and he was the only child of older folk who were deeply grateful for the arrival of their son, festooning their love upon him, and believing that he was the answer to their many years of prayer.

Pierre was a loving son, a diligent student and a devoted Christian, so much so that his parents felt deeply grateful when he eventually became a candidate for holy orders on his nineteenth birthday.

Pierre's father worked on a prosperous arable farm, and was part of a workforce with several fellow labourers, who also had sons. Pierre developed a clandestine love affair with one of these boys, which lasted for a year, and which he described as being an utterly blissful period of deep communion.

Then suddenly, paradise ceased, as the father of the boy found further employment in southern France, moving the family to the new region. Pierre was devastated, and experienced a period of traumatic abandonment, eased only by his devotional life, his connection with nature, and the mystical nature of visions.

One day as he walked across a field to Church, he saw an Angel who spoke to him. The Angel gave its name as Gabriel, and communicating through a language of light, provided Pierre with a series of powerful revelations — visions that concerned changes within the world order — and how Pierre would give his life in service.

These transcendent meetings continued over a period of three months, during which seven teachings were revealed, revelations that he would later use in the ministry of his healing. Whilst in prayer the last Angelic encounter occurred one day, and a hugely powerful transmission of light entered his body, after which he became unconscious. Pierre believed an hour had passed whilst he 'slept'.

After receiving this last oracular transmission, Pierre remembered waking to the sensation of his aura being vastly extended and within a field of light, a force he believed that emanated from the Divine. He saw light pouring from his hands and heart, and knew that he must use this energy for the healing he had been informed about, through the in-tuition of the seven teachings.

It was then that his profound faith in God led him through a sequence of synchronous events to the Dominican brotherhood.

The community took him as theirs, providing him with order, succour and purpose, and yet whilst in candidature he was told to not use his healing abilities. Indeed, he was altogether asked to completely refrain from talking about his Angelic teachings.

As the years passed Pierre became extremely frustrated and depressed within the order, for he was deeply moved by the nature of the creation story he had been given by the Angel. And with regard to his sexuality, he felt that the manifestation of God inherent in the world must be a sacred union between the male and female principles.

This was paradigm that did not correspond with the canonical law of the Dominican order. Many confusions concerning dogma encouraged him into feeling disaffected from the community that had once succoured him, and after a number of years of pain he decided to remit his orders.

On leaving the order, Pierre spiralled into a deeper depression. All that he had held precious, all that had cushioned him, all that had given purpose to his temporal and spiritual existence had seemingly diminished. This included the healing power transmitted from his hands which he knew had been divinely bestowed.

At our meeting it was apparent that Pierre needed to be energetically 'rebooted', his energy field was clear to see and yet was in turmoil. Pierre's aura was extremely porous, and torn in several places as a result of repressing the fire-fed passions that moved the very core of his existence.

For so long he had held back the power of his physical love of life, and we created a strategy, working on the very sensitive aspect of his light field, and initially transmuting the emotional body attachments — to loss, abandonment, guilt and isolation — concerning his sexuality. We identified each unresolved issue, committing much to prayer and asking the Angels for profound healing. Then a miracle occurred.

One night Pierre dreamt he was once again with Archangel Gabriel, and on this occasion was surrounded by a number of other Angels, including other nature spirits or elementals. On waking, he experienced an extremely high fever that lasted for three days, and which burned off much of the negativity he had identified, after which he felt elated, as though all the sensations of woe, loss and depression had transmuted into joy.

Suffice to say Pierre is now practicing his own powerful healing art, is at peace with his sexuality, and reconnected with the devotional pathway of daily prayer, meditation and chanting. Believing in the ritual of pilgrimage, he has found that a journey to a sacred site on each Equinox and Solstice has enhanced his dedication.

In Conclusion...

For centuries sacraments similar to those above have been practised in our world's major spiritual centres. Such devotional disciplines expand our spiritual muscle, organize our emotional intelligence, and enhance our allegiance to that we consider most pure and with God.

Although each step maybe easily identified, the work must be taken as a ritual, whereby we allow its information to reform our whole being, to seep deep into our physical presence by the experience of confronting all that stops us from being authentic. For the authentic self, is the source of personal fulfilment and the soul's nourishment. Otherwise, however we identify the task without ritual, it merely remains within our intellect as a notion, not as a sensation.

We have all read as many of the spiritual or self-help books that we can accumulate, in order to feel good. Often we brandish the latest technology defined by our intellects, to score social points for how spiritual we are, and yet are we truly living the word, are we fully defined in our celestial conduct?

In order to be fully initiated, we must pass through a daily ritual as an offering to the divine within us. To offer ourselves in this way is an act of love, and a point of transition in the co-creativity of the outer plane we know as planetary order.

The sacraments offered above were given by the Angels of Atlantis to specifically help us with this act, to make robust our commitment to this golden age we are at this time creating, by the very act of dwelling within these words as posterns of courage and joy. For these attainments were similarly achieved many thousands of years ago in Atlantis, and defined by divine beings working in association with the Angels to create heaven on earth. This they did, and this we may also do.

CHAPTER FIVE

†HE HEAR† ΛΠGELS

*The intuition of the heart
is the super-highway where the Angels roam.*
 - RUPERT SHELDRAKE

In the Middle East there exists an old legend. The story tells how the Infinite One made a statue of clay in the image of his/her own likeness, and asked the Soul to enter it, yet the Soul refused. To be captured thus meant sure imprisonment, and the Soul's essence was to be free and joyous, liberated on the wings of its own triumphal ecstasy.

However, God, in infinite wisdom asked the heavenly host of Angels to sing Seraphic music, and the Soul was so *enchanted*, so deeply stirred by the celestial sound, that the Soul agreed to enter the body of clay.

So began Adam Kadmon. So began the origin of human life.

Angels and Celestial Spirits have always existed. Their lives abound with acts of genuine kindness, healing and ubiquitous support of humanity. Wherever they may be, they are linked to the most powerful force within the universe, the vibrational currency of love and joy. Thus, they are encoded with the passion and praise of God's love richly within their hearts, and so they live the beauty of the great song that once enchanted life into existence.

Human acts of charity, inspired by the Angels, are on the increase during this time of unfolding, as we shift consciousness from the love of power to the power of love. So, it is with this conviction that I wish to open an Angelic Pathway, to explore the different faces of angelic countenance, and to acknowledge the reflection of the Divine, in both the human and celestial messengers of light. In this we help form the fabric of transformative consciousness within the Universe that exists throughout the many dimensions of living light, and in turn we are moved to love all - including those who appear to not drink of the light.

In this time of gestation, in this period of quickening when many of us are awakening to the existence of Spirit, and are conscious of the living connective tissue of the universe -this is the time when we may be inspired by levels of existence beyond the material world, meaning those not created by human thought alone.

Both modern cosmology and ancient angelology give credence to Ambassadors from the celestial realms. This occurs, either through the photographic appearance of photons of light as elementary particles, suffusing time and space with rare and often miraculous angelic orbs, or other happenings — by the experience of Angelic messengers appearing by the bedside of someone profoundly sick or dying, or by visions occurring as remarkable sightings in social gatherings – most of which have enchanted the faithful.

However, the current wave of activity concerning celestial spheres, orbs, angelic flames or winged creatures of Seraphic proportion, is not new. These appearances have been present before, throughout many stations of time. Indeed, Angelic activity in the West reaches us through a series of powerful ancient vectors, arising from the mystical pathways within the major spiritual disciplines of Christianity, Judaism and Islam.

For example, in the Bible one can read many extraordinary stories about Angelic appearance, as in Psalm 8 when it is stated: *"You have made humans a little less than the angels."* Whereas, in the Koran we read: *"The Angel Gabriel said: For every letter that a man reads of the sacred word, God will create an Angel that shall plant a tree for him in paradise."* Lastly in this brief exposition, the Torah has written: *"He who seeks to ascend to the palaces of the heavens and to achieve a vision of glory, will need to pass the angelic guardians."*

Angels are with us now, just as they were in ancient times. They are omnipresent, and through surveys I have conducted whilst facilitating The Alchemy Of Voice workshops, I've discovered that seventy-five percent of the people who attend believe in the possibility of Angels, and have experienced indirect Angelic manifestations in more than one situation. Whilst twenty-five per cent of the people attending suggest they have had a direct experience of the angelic order in the form of a presence that often defies human description.

Greek And Roman Angels

In ancient Greek and Roman society, a common belief was that Angels abounded in the form of divine attendants: in Greece, citizens believed that a person's life was supported by a 'Daemon', and in Rome a 'Genius'. These mostly unseen beings were the Angelic guides, or Spirit guardians, whose consciousness was powerfully linked with the soul or higher self of the person they attended, and through this agency it was commonly believed that Angels aided the outcome of all significant actions.

Angels are the thought messengers of God, and as glimpses of the Divine, present themselves to human life in order to help create loving outcomes in any situation, major or minor. They provide physical and emotional support in the only way possible, by expecting nothing in return, and whenever spiritual nourishment is specifically required. You see Angels love for the sake of love, whereas human beings love for the sake of being loved.

In ancient times it was believed that each act of creation was lit from within by these Divine Geniis, and that their inspired wisdom poured through humanity into the material world of form. All artists sought or indeed waited for a time when their Muse or Angel came forth in order to create. The belief was that these magical, divine entities would light the fire that literally inspired the work into creation, and that creative genius was merely on loan from the divine. It was believed that in these moments of unique creation, humanity met the great mystery of God through the Angels: such as we hear at the beginning of *Henry V* by William Shakespeare:

> *"O for a muse of fire that would ascend,*
> *The brightest heaven of invention,*
> *And let us ciphers to this great account*
> *On your imaginary forces work."*
> ~ *HENRY V*

Everyday Angelic Appearance

Angels emerge in the daily experience of men and women throughout the world's cultures. Indeed, most societies acknowledge the existence of spirits at a level beyond the human. In the West we have grown very familiar with these unique phenomena helping and assisting our daily processes, although in other world cultures Angels exist through other various spiritual identities. For example, in Native America, Angels are referred to as Elementals or Spirits, and throughout Hinduism and Buddhism, aren't specifically labelled, and are simply seen as emanations of spiritual force, particularly that of the natural world, the great Devas.

Whatever human perception may offer, Angels are Angels, and are non-denominational, existing as primordial beings arising from the thoughts of God in order, through great loving action, to assist and remind us that our hearts are the seat of our souls.

Angels in Antiquity

Angels in their legions are mentioned throughout the Bible, and in most medieval Cathedrals, Churches, Abbeys, Burgers or Town Halls, are depicted in close harmony with the Cosmos and all living things. Angels playing instruments in praise of the Divine was a common medieval viewpoint, because Angels were alive to the people who created the great centres of spiritual learning and temporal power.

In the Bible there are numerous allusions to the creative action of Angels governing the Universe, and they are closely linked with service to the Christos: the celestial force that upholds the cosmic messages of Love, Peace, Unity and Compassion.

Similarly, Angelic manifestations were recorded in the great writings of the Christian Mystics, such as Thomas Aquinas, Saint John of the Cross and Hildegard von Bingen.

Futhermore in the Koran, Angels are accorded the privilege of being one of the six articles of faith: *"If there were settled on earth Angels, walking about in peace and quiet, we should certainly have sent them down from the heavens; angels are messengers."*

Angels And The Cosmos

Angels are beings of light whose purpose is to serve solely through loving action, and yet they are destined to perform many acts of service, for again, Angels love for the sake of loving, whilst human beings love for the sake of being loved.

The word *Angel* is derived from the Greek Angelos: meaning 'messenger of light', and as such they move with great velocity throughout the Cosmos, even faster than light. For their key role is to pass between the worlds, obeying the directions of the Divine in service to the consciousness of humanity and the Planet Earth, and in this they are supremely patient, understanding beings. Angels live to feel, whereas human beings seek to know. Therefore, Angels do not need schooling as humans do. They know the essence of everything through intuition, for intuition is the soul of every thought, and the super highway that carries their particular magic. Indeed, Angels and Artists have always been closely connected, creating muse-based relationships, and bringing forth the magical language of artistic expression. For beauty is an emanation of the Divine, and uplifts us to inspirational strength when we are down.

Angels And Art

In the 15th century, Fra Angelico (Brother Giovanni, the Angelic One) painted fragile, delicate images of these celestial beings, believing that each image he had was made more real through artistic representation. Just as during the Industrial Revolution of mid-nineteenth century England, Edward Burne-Jones reported: *"When they make another machine, I'll paint another Angel."*

Angels are inspirational for they live within the hosting vibration of divine will, and as such their knowledge is the vibration of the heart. Knowing, loving, prophecy and praising are their expressions, and in this they teach us of the evolutionary force within the cosmos. Indeed, they are profusely seen in Renaissance Art holding large trumpets, praising God and jubilant in adoration - just as they do in the Hallelujah chorus.

Praise Crisis

If we live in a world where there is no praise, in a world that is run by machines and technology alone, our bodies are literally sucked dry of joy. In their omniscience, angels know this and appear at this dawning of Aquarius to release us from potential crisis. Thousands of years ago, St. Paul wrote:

*"If I speak in the tongues of mortals and angels but do not have
Love…I am a noisy gong or a clanging cymbal.
If I have prophetic powers,
And understand all the mysteries
And all knowledge…
If I have Faith, so as to remove mountains, but do not have Love…
I am nothing."*

Praise is the sound that awe and joy make when they meet together, and as such are powerful emanations of Divine magic. Happiness always arrests us when we apprehend something greater than ourselves: *"For a man's reach should always exceed his grasp or what's heaven for,"* wrote Robert Browning.

This conviction opens our hearts to their joy-filled song of love, and so we transform the disguise we have worn for many years in the denial of our soul. For we Human Angels were seeded beyond the mists of time, to act as Guardians to those who have forgotten who they truly are. We were coded to awaken the true nature of every human being here on earth as a soul-filled presence.

When we fully become this, we activate our sacred connection with the planet as a vehicle of life in the evolution of the Cosmos. As we live this in each moment, we assist the Christ consciousness of the planet. Thus, we encourage a vast inter-dimensional shift to take place, and the seal that was placed on our soul's knowledge millennia ago is removed. So, the suit of the old disguise melts from our bodies. For it is time to praise, it is time to open our Heart's Note, and therefore to enhance the acceleration of our DNA.

Our potential is vast, and it is prophesied that through the foreseeable future as intelligent life forms on this planet, we have the inherent ability to evolve a triple helix DNA, with the advanced possibility of developing twelve strands. As we evolve to this degree, each of the seven Chakras, combined with the first transpersonal energy centre the Eighth Chakra of the Christos, resonates with such fusion that we develop 'wings of light' allowing us to soar with the divine.

The Eighth Chakra is the chakra of unity consciousness, and when open, a suffusion of light pours from the upper energy centres, and the aura expands, filled with supernal light – just as we see in medieval paintings of the Saints and Angels.

Angelic Encounters

Story One: Delivery Of The Crystal Children

A client of mine told me this wonderful story about meeting emissaries from the Angelic kingdom, and her relationship to the twin boys she gave birth to. The children were deeply desired, and had been intuitively part of her consciousness for much of her life. So, when Elizabeth eventually gave birth to Jasper and Cosmo, there was much joyous celebration.

During her childhood Elizabeth had dreamed an extremely lucid dream, in which she met a guardian Angel. Elizabeth wholeheartedly believed this was Archangel Gabriel. The dream consisted of being in a large, light-filled room that was also intensified by beautiful soft harmonics.

The music appeared to be more vibration than made by instruments, and moved with waving shafts of coloured light that filled the whole space. The ambience of the room was ecstatic, filled with a quality of love that seemed to literally hang in the air.

Elizabeth felt herself floating to a large cushion, and was spoken to by three Angels that appeared from the light. The Angels foretold that Elizabeth would be Mother to twin souls that would incarnate as boys. Again, their language appeared more as light than sound, although she heard that she would witness three signs in her life that would herald the meeting, conception, and awakening of these souls in human form.

At this point, the three Angels fused into one powerful beam of light that Elizabeth was initially frightened of before moving into awe ~ a wave of extraordinary love light that pulsated from within a single beam, and the form of an Orb emerged like a figure of incandescence. The figure appeared to hold great loving pulsations of light within it and wrapped a wave of consciousness around the space in which she as a young girl sat.

The Angel said its name was Gabriel, and that she would live in dedication of serving her fellow beings through the knowledge of love, and that her children would be great teachers in their own right, and at this point she woke up.

As Elizabeth matured she developed a keen intelligence and having attended University, graduated with a high status degree, after which she gained employment in the business community. These years brought challenge and growth, and then fifteen years into her career she experienced a major incident.

Whilst driving home from work late one winter's evening, the car she was driving swerved on ice and hit a tree. The car was severely damaged, and Elizabeth narrowly escaped losing her life. The injuries she sustained were considerable, and a major fracture in the upper right femur bone, meant the likelihood of her never successfully conceiving children.

Throughout her recovery Elizabeth continued to believe in the dream-filled prophecy she had received as a child, and even though she had not experienced any other visitation, intimation or intuition from her guardian Angel, she simply knew that in some way she would have children.

During the latter stages of her recuperation in hospital, a recovery that staggered the entire medical team, Elizabeth met a handsome Physiotherapist called Charles. Their work together was intense, and her recovery was immediate, through which Elizabeth gained full motor control of her once shattered hip whilst relearning how to walk.

A strong feeling of profound intimacy developed between them, and Elizabeth often referred to the blonde-haired, blue-eyed Charles as her human Angel.

However, when it came time to leave hospital, Elizabeth learned that Charles had to visit aging parents living in another country, and so they lost touch.

Elizabeth regained her job status, albeit working more as a Consultant, and five years passed. Then one morning as she walked from a cab to her office building, she mistakenly dropped a book, which was immediately picked up by a man. Her physiotherapist Charles just happened to be passing down the major street where her new office was, en route to a meeting. They again became transfixed by each other and arranged to meet later that day. After a short period of time, they regained the profound intimacy they had once cherished. The relationship blossomed, and soon they were living together, when Elizabeth began experiencing acute dreams about the guardian angel she had experienced 30 years previously. On the night of the third dream, Elizabeth felt utterly certain that she was pregnant, contradicting the medical information she had been given.

Months later, and on the night when the birth contractions began, the room became filled with the same ambient love, light and music she had experienced in her dream as a child - all was sublime and supernal.

Charles also felt this divine radiance, and when the children were born, they and the space, were bathed in the exquisite nature of the light and harmony. In the midst of this force, Elizabeth once more felt the presence of her guardian Angel providing her with such love that the labour of bringing forth the two babes was made easy.

The night after the birth took place Elizabeth was again visited by Archangel Gabriel. In these moments she knew her quest was fulfilled, the prophecy granted, and the knowledge imbued. Her sons were destined to become spiritual teachers, as the Archangel suggested the children were Crystal Ray creations, and that deep within their genetic coding was fifth dimensional force from the Angelic kingdom. Later in life, as they matured, they would speak their cosmic message to the world, for their incarnations were in alignment with earth energy developments.

Story Two: Angels Pass Over

In 1980 my Mother died at the age of sixty. Having lived through several battles with Cancer, the last took her. Kathleen or Kay, as her intimates knew her, was a special kind of person: filled with positivism, eternally loving, incessantly in service to her fellows, and always questing information that she saw was innovative or 'with-it'.

When she perished, having lived much longer than the prediction of her physicians, it was a sacred release. At last the pain was finished, at last the dull ache of serial medication was removed, at last the anguish of death no longer stalked like the Grim Reaper, and the final breath out was an anthem of freedom.

But, it cost those who watched. With terrible tears and aching hearts we mourned her loss, and although I wasn't present at her final moment, I was at death's prelude, and I had looked after her through the bitter final months.

The last night was extraordinary, even though for the first time in her illness Kay accepted she was dying, and a dreadfully mournful sense of departure was present. Suddenly, the entire room became filled with shafts of Angelic light, championed by Zadkiel ~ the Angel of Compassion.

It seemed that Kay was levitated by the light, held by loving wings, and succoured by the knowledge of the Divine Mother that poured through into her bedroom, and it was in this moment that my Mother asked me to take her to Hospital, to die.

Kay was conscious, albeit filled with morphine, and I was able to lift her into my waiting car and drive her past the places that she had loved so well in life, constantly surrounded by the awesome light of Zadkiel and her other spirit guides. Once we were at the Hospital, she was gathered by another loving presence in the form of the kind Nurses. This was when she slipped into unconsciousness and twelve hours later passed into spirit.

Angels soothe us to our rest, guide us to soul's learning, and breathe protective currents of balm into our hearts and weary bodies. Their love is sublime.

How To Comprehend Heart Angels

Many people are moving from doubt concerning the possibility of interacting with angels. Our belief in the intuition of the heart as a super-highway means our sensitivity is being tuned. The postscripts of the European Industrial Revolution that gave us great advances in technology but also undermined so much of our extra-sensory awareness, particularly with regard to the principles of intuition, finer sensing and harmony, are being healed. Through studying the symbolism and mythology of any of our ancient civilizations, one finds alive the central principles of grace and truth. All great civilizations sought to express themselves through these precepts: signalling that human moral order, the natural world, and cosmic force, are interrelated and interdependent-that all nature leans towards harmony and is rooted in wholeness.

Human nature always seeks the path of least resistance, seeking its own liberation, and is innately spiritual, desiring to know the origin and purpose of all things. So as we move through these extraordinary cycles of natural evolution, our sensibilities open to the intuitive mind as a sacred gift, and we are made aware of the Angelic Realms, and the Elemental or Devic Spirits, as agencies that can truly assist us in times that are a'changing.

Archangel Sona Meditation

- Make sure you have Silence, Solitude and Stillness.
- Prepare the way for an Archangelic Transmission by entering your Sacred Space and closing the door.
- Sit with an aligned spine, feeling your weight, and assume a Mudra by bringing your thumb and forefinger together on each hand ~ the latter connects powerful energies within, associated with the moon and sun.
- Firstly, empty all of your breath out through your lips, wait for a moment to feel the need to breathe, and then breathe in. As you feel the Prana fill your being, see the energy as a coloured force, see the breath as light filling your being, moving down your spine as an elevator descends through a shaft. Then sigh out.
- Repeat the breathing process, in and out *seven* times, but on these occasions hum the breath out to the last moment of its conviction. Allow the hum to be centred in your heart, which evokes its force. Angelic transmissions always arise from the essence of love, and so be with this intention as you breathe in and out and *HUM*. Be with the breath-light arising from the Angelic Realms and entering into the secret chamber of your heart.
- Pause for a moment, and notice the delicious stillness that wraps your energy field ~ you may hear a ringing in your inner ear, feel a gracious presence, you may see a gold, silver or mother-of-pearl light in the air. For when we evoke the Angels their energies permeate the atmosphere of the place we inhabit. They fill us with the light of joy!
- Now, take another breath and tuning into the Earth element found in your pelvic area, chant EL for as long as the breath will sustain it.

- Whilst chanting this mantra think of Archangel Uriel who is responsible for the element of the EARTH, we will sound EL three times.
- Then, move to the solar plexus and chant EEM through three sustained breaths. This chant evokes the Water element, whose custodian is Archangel Gabriel.
- Then, chant OM on three sustained breaths in the throat chakra. This evokes the AIR element, whose custodian is Archangel Raphael.
- Finally, chant KA three times through the crown chakra, which evokes the Fire element of Archangel Michael. PAUSE.

- The chant of EL EEM OM KA is derived from other dimensions, and received intuitively from the Archangelic realms. You will feel a shift of frequency. It is very powerful, and so you might feel either highly sensitive, or a shift of consciousness through the whole of your being.
- Whatever you may feel, remember this is completely within your governance, as you are the master/mistress of your own destiny. In the words of the poet W.E.Henley:
    "I am the master of my Fate
    I am the captain of my Soul."
- Simply be still for a moment or two, noticing how the energies dance around you and within you and any discomfort will pass. Once the energies have re-balanced your genetic code, you will feel illuminated by a golden light within and without. At this point, whatever you are sensing, see yourself protected in a golden sheath, sealing your force and connecting with the elemental force. The gold is an insulating device from the Archangelic kingdoms – it is very powerful energy to use. Observe the space and much will come to you.
- When using this mantra, people often see a brightly lit spiralling force, vertically ascending and descending. The spiral is often formed of rainbow colours, flashing and shimmering fractal patterns, rather similar to the dream recorded in Genesis of Jacob's ladder.
- There is a belief that the spiralling nature of these energies reflects the essence of the DNA double helix, and the constant circling of energies that we find in the essence of nature—like water running down a hole, the spiral pattern of seashells, or the spirals that govern the shape of the Milky Way. These are of the Source, and therefore divinely inspired.
- When we use this mantra as a talisman, it will open a sense of your Guardian Angel, or a visitation from the Archangels themselves.

Developing Intuition Through Extra-Sensory Perception

During Angelic encounters it is highly likely that you will feel enhanced intuition, or a vibration that affects your whole being. This largely occurs because the Angel's light-filled body affects vast change within your own light body, which will download into your physical body, allowing you to feel extra sensory processes taking place. If you are concerned, say a prayer of love and light, and you will feel automatically comforted about the following:

CLAIRVOYANCE ~ seeing energy or force through light, colour, form or image - the holy ones, including our spirit guides, download their communications to us through our finer sensing. *Do you particularly perceive through vision?*

CLAIRAUDIENCE ~ hearing the sound of a rushing force, or a high/low pitch frequency are possible phenomena that precede spiritual visitations. Often people hear voices (not the voices that occur through delusional behaviour, when the individual may be psychologically unwell; if this is so, please meet with a learned Counsel) that can be the voices of dear, departed ones, or the directions of an Angelic Guardian. In the case of the latter you will probably register the voice as your own higher self, affirming that a certain action needs to be taken. *Do you predominantly perceive through hearing?*

CLAIRSENTIENCE ~ this is when all of our senses receive the frequency of energy emerging from phenomena: we hear, feel, see, smell or taste the vibration. My experience of the rarefied force of Angelic activity suggests that all the senses are brought into perceiving these extraordinary celestial messengers. However, this statement must not preclude what is appropriate for you: *Do you feel the whole of your being opened to full sentience?*

Develop these tools for perceiving the preternatural world by meeting regularly with a Spiritual Teacher, a friend or a group of 'like-minded' individuals. The most accurate vibration is the most important, and so manifest someone or a group of people who are a vibrational match for you. Regular sonic meditation exercises will help you accomplish extra-sensory perception.

There are many ways of accomplishing this degree of heart-centred psyche. Some people use pendulums, dowsing, tarot cards, scrying lustrous pools of water, aura reading, sounding or toning, symbol ministrations, tea leaf/coffee reading, singing bowls, tuning forks or bell ringing, drumming, candle gazing or crystal ball watching. All these techniques are traditional tools used in the mystery schools for concentrating the mind to 'see'.

All are tools for magic, for the ability to 'feel' between the levels of dimensional experience, to apperceive energy that is parallel with or interwoven between the three dimensionality of our world. Opening in this way will enable the spiritual initiate to sensitize more fully to a meeting with the Angels. But remember all is achieved by simply being the thought, and then by following the whisperings of your higher self or intuition.

Meeting Your Guardian Angel

If you wish to commune with your Guardian Angel, or indeed with any of the Archangels, it is important to sanctify a place in your heart, and then within the space around you. This is like preparing for an esteemed guest, when we adorn our house or the temple in preparation. This heartfelt intention enables us to magnetize the fullness and purity of Angelic benediction.

Find your own sacred space, which may be your own sacred temple, room or a natural landscape, a place of great beauty that vibrates a higher frequency for you, and somewhere that is adorned in stillness. Organize your thoughts in the sense of what you request of the Angelic presence, allowing the thoughts to vibrate through the whole of your body, and make sure that your physical constitution is clear by drinking pure water.

Light a candle and burn frankincense to especially purify the space and yourself, and as you enter that special zone of asking and receiving, still yourself through being grounded. Use the heart vowel AH, or sing the OM, as they prepare our vibration for the exquisite rays of the Divine presence.

Then utter this prayer:

Dear Guardian Angel (use their name if you have identified one):
Please hear my supplication as I yield in loving awe of your exquisite nature, to the heartfelt power of your love and compassion.
Please fold me in your wings of tender light.
Please receive my thanks for all that you have watched over in my life, particularly when I have not been vigilant to your divine presence.

Please grant me the power of your charity, as I seek the will to
[use appropriate expression for you] _____

Please fill my heart with the wisdom of infinite love, and fill my soul with divine radiance.

Please heal my wounds, so that I may heal others.

Please teach me celestial knowledge so that I may embody kindness, and radiate unconditional love for all my brothers and sisters.

So be it.

Amen.

Feeling The Angelic Realms

When you are in the presence of the Angelic realms you may:

- feel warm and protected as though held by pure, loving all-oneness
- feel the room or space around you suddenly become very still or silent, as though time and space are expanding
- hear a high pitched harmonic, or ringing sound that suggests a frequency change within and without your being. This is a shift to a higher harmonic frequency
- feel the temperature or pressure of air change
- feel as though you are held by a quality of great safety, even if the Angelic presence is warning you of negativity
- smell a scent of flowers, incense, or as though a dear departed one's scent is nigh
- feel that the experience is awesomely real
- feel as though you are being touched or caressed by unseen energies, particularly in the upper body area ~your head or shoulders
- feel slightly 'spacey', as though you are about to fall asleep
- feel an adrenaline rush for no apparent reason
- feel suddenly very clear about a problem that you were hitherto unable to solve
- feel completely resolved about a life issue or challenge
- feel surrounded by a sense that you know so well, and yet cannot fully identify
- see lights flickering in the space around you, particularly through your peripheral vision, or in shafts of golden or silver light like rain
- feel amazingly positive and empowered

What Do You Feel?

On the other hand, if you are sensing a negative astral presence, which is not from the Angelic realm of fifth, sixth or seventh dimensional counsel, you may:

- feel very negative or angry
- feel very cold and irritated
- feel as though your skin itches
- feel fearful or a sense of panic
- feel a sense of alone-ness
- feel a sense of desperation

If you are experiencing any of the above negativities, please light a candle, ring a bell, and hold up a sacred image. Be with a totem or divine talisman that is a power tool for you, and say this prayer:

> *Dear Archangel Michael,*
> *Please wrap me in your wings of protective light.*
> *From the centre where the will of God is known, please allow the plan of light to flow, and seal the door where darkness dwells.*
> *From the kingdom that is utmost love and peace, please draw the Christ filled light to me.*
> *May all peace and love be made free.*
> *May the love of the Divine Mother Mary fill our hearts with radiance.*
> *So Be It.*
> *Amen.*

Calling upon Archangel Michael, the wise leader of the heavenly host brings with it a powerful charge that will dispel any measure of negativity. However, if you continue to be troubled, remember that this process is under your entire management. The force only occurs if you have a vibrational match with it, so communicate with the energy to discern its identity, or consult with an energy healer, therapist or shaman.

How To Identify Your Heart Angel

There are myriad Angels. Often their names can be revealed through past or present, and each earth-culture varies their Angelic naming. The significant thing is to feel and know what is intuitively accurate for you.

The Infinite One is constantly creating Angels that arise to serve our evolution. There are Angels that look after Cosmic Ordering, Planetary Evolution, Elemental Science, the interface between living intelligence and artificial intelligence, Quantum Physics, Fractal time, the Nature Kingdom, and Human life.

Angels have been traditionally organized into hierarchies for time immemorial, and their ranking was tabulated in prayerful teachings by a Syrian Christian Mystic known as Dionysius the Areopagite, in the sixth century:

First Sphere: Heavenly Counsellors

1. Seraphim
2. Cherubim
3. Thrones

Second Sphere: Heavenly Governors

4. Dominions
5. Virtues
6. Powers

Third Sphere: Heavenly Messengers

7. Principalities
8. Archangels
9. Angels

Angels are Non-hierarchical

However, the Angels of Atlantis, my specific Angelic guides have asked us to consider a movement away from the notion of hierarchy. Often when we become preoccupied with the notion of hierarchies, we place prejudice upon our choices, rather than seeing the unique role of each Angelic entity. In the 'new world' order, these roles will exist as multilateral vibrations. We will see power structures change, as the essence of love and compassion become apparent as fully lived objectives, as the 'word is made flesh full of grace and truth', we will see organizations shift their power.

The pyramid order creating the hierarchy of the past, arising from Patriarchal governance, will shift, is shifting into the use of lateral management processes, where each person feels themselves to be a valuable sum of the whole. This means that human beings will be aware of their individual choice in each moment, chosen through emotional and spiritual intelligence, fully cognizant of the energy boundaries that create radically embodied truth, and full of respect for each another. Thus a powerful new paradigm is born.

As human beings evolve, as we adjust to the dawning of Aquarius, openhearted emotional intelligence will lead us to behaviour that is led by love, empathy, patience and unity. Thereby, each living entity will recognize its co-creative role in the world and the cosmos.

To comprehend sacred Holarchy in opposition to a Hierarchy (even though the word hierarchy means *the rule of the sacred*, and in modern times has shifted in meaning to the rule of the elite) and to apprehend divine assistance through Angelic consciousness, we may see how the elements of earth, water, air and fire support the superhighway through which the Angels roam. This differentiates without the inference of status.

THE ANGELIC ELEMENT OF FIRE

This is a force of vibration closest to the Source and the kingdom of the Seraphim, Cherubim and Thrones. The Seraphs and Cherubs are seen respectively as God's immediate vessels of light-filled instruction. They burn with the brightest zeal, with the greatest intensity, and with the all-consuming creative life force.

Indeed, the name Seraphim in Hebrew means "those who kindle or make hot", and the word Cherubim "those who burn to protect in the fullness of knowledge". The Cherubim are seen stationed at the gates of the Garden of Eden. These lustrous ones directly receive divine illumination, which pours from their beings as they surround the throne of God. Bestowing love as they do, our hearts are made hot by their continuous Praise, for they filter profound intelligence to us concerning new of ways of governance – whether this be personal or societal.

THE ANGELIC ELEMENT OF AIR

This kingdom governs mental intelligence, and is the dominion for organizing creation on a fundamental level. This is the realm of the Archangels who serve as master architects, assisting the concordance of the divine plan through the blueprint of their consciousness. Their role governs the means by which our planetary systems function.

Calling in Archangelic aid creates powerful change, and so leaders of anointed rank, such as Presidents and Sovereigns are often fully assisted by these majestic beings of Light. Therefore, these Angels bring about changes that benefit the whole of humanity.

THE ANGELIC ELEMENT OF WATER

This dimension is the emotional plane, the element that brings the radiation of feeling into existence. This vibration is a fluid account of the Angels that we usually meet in the form of Guardians or Helpers, during times of great personal travail. Of course, all divine messengers serve humanity by tending to the 'heart' of humanity, and yet the Angel sightings that abound at this time of monumental change are visitations from these particular divine ones.

THE ANGELIC ELEMENT OF EARTH

As we journey through the Angelic realms, we reach the kingdom of the Deva or Nature Spirits who serve as guardians of the natural world, and therefore bring goodness to the function of what is borne on earth. Their roles are elaborate in service to the Angelic kingdoms and consist of:

- Unicorns ~ Angel messengers of pure rank: they work with the souls of human beings.
- Dryads - tree or wood spirits.
- Sylphs ~ air spirits.
- Naiads and Undines ~ water spirits.
- Salamanders ~ fire spirits.
- Elves, Fairies, Pixies, Brownies, Goblins, Leprechauns, and Dwarves are earth spirits who tend the different harmonic levels by nourishing the natural world.

The Art Of Calling In The Archangels And Hearing Heaven's Message

The more we call upon the power of the Angelic kingdoms, the more we meditate on their exquisite energies, the more we beseech Angelic aid - the more we feel their ultimate effect in our lives.

Remember their energy is ubiquitous, and our personal frequency has become unused to their refined transmission, so by regularly tuning to meditation, chant and prayer, we may more easily become part of the intuitive super highway where they roam.

Moreover, as we reconnect with their sublime force, extraordinary miracles abound: shifts of perception sharpen our sensing, and link us with stellar information that enriches our process bringing about greater faith.

Divine transmissions often take the form of:

- Visioning Angelic energy through shapes, Lights or Orbs, and discovering feathers on one's path anywhere and everywhere.
- Increased synchronicity ~ the experience of two or more events which are not causally related, and occur in a meaningful fashion. The most common form of synchronicity is that you think about someone, and then they are encountered in an unlikely place.
- Being drawn to the images of Angels in architecture, stained glass windows, books, magazines or greeting cards. Or, you may receive direct transmissions from Angelic countenance itself.
- By listening to high vibrational music, particularly that which was created during the period of cultural renaissance in the west, when Angelology was alive and abundant in peoples' lives. Sacred music and sacred voice were experienced as transcendent corridors to the divine, and so will uplift your force by their harmonies. Listen to William Byrd, Thomas Tallis, Monteverdi and Palestrina's liturgical music. These composers base the work on the harmonic sequences that elevate consciousness and connect with the Angels.
- By feeling a deep desire for Stillness and personal reflection, whether this is in your personal living space, or in a beautiful natural landscape. The SSS code (silence, solitude and stillness) provides a movement away from the 'noise' of our lives (those electrical charges that disharmonize our health), and thus we are re-united with the space of soul in which we live, but rarely 'be with'. Whenever we move into the quality of this stillness, and ask, angel messages arise plentifully.
- Archangels are motivated by the vibration of these processes because they look after our hearts.

On the following pages are the names and qualities of the Archangels who gave me "The Alchemy Of Voice" – a Temple of Sound Healing practiced in both Atlantis and Egypt, and restored today by this work.

The Heart Archangels ~
Messages from Heaven

GABRIEL
Sacred Name: **Messenger of God**
Divine Action: **God is my strength**
Colour Ray: **Blue**
Mineral Stone: **Lapis Lazuli**
Essence: **Myrrh**

Gabriel's strength, inspiration and purpose bring forth powerful messages to Earth directly from God. We may read of this loving service in the story of Mohammad receiving the Koran, with Gabriel (as it were) taking dictation directly from Divine Thought.

Similarly, there is the story of Mary receiving 'a calling' from Gabriel that she would conceive of a child named Jeshua. This child would be the Son of God, and he would bring love from the kingdom of heaven to all men.

Whenever a major life transition occurs for you, and you need help with your dreams, aspirations and projects, Gabriel will always be ready to bring blessed messages. This Archangel will help to bring succour, and to shine light on your path. By divine benediction Gabriel helps to create balance and grace and so we may beseech this Archangelic messenger thus:

Enchanting And Invoking God's Messenger:

Dear Archangel Gabriel,
I pray for loving guidance, great Messenger.
As I meet my life's creative pathway, please provide me with the light of your presence, so that I may clearly see the highest choice through your message.
I am willing to change anything in me to bring forth clarity, love and light.
Oh dear Gabriel please initiate my seeing, so as to remove the obstacles of my fear.
ELEEMOMKA
So be it.
Amen.

HANAEL
Sacred Name: **The Sacred Warrior**
Divine Action: **Glory of the Divine**
Colour Ray: **Red**
Mineral Stone: **Ruby**
Essence: **Geranium**

When we meet the Archangels they come with a powerful light. Their divine emission stirs us to the truth in our lives. Their energies are vital, tenacious, fully luminous and sometimes intensely 'blinding', and with this force they tap our inner sensing in order to awaken our heart's purpose, particularly when our life's path is misdirected.

Hanael is one such force, bringing into focus our purpose and strength, through a sense of direction created by courage and hope. Therefore, living with this Angel will encourage you through revelation, to change your creative path when you are not fully aligned with an open regard for your incarnation.

Archangels like Hanael intuitively sense what is to be, and scan the Akashic Hall of Records. When we ask for their assistance, their laser powers assert our belief in love, freedom, compassion, harmony, beauty, integrity and wisdom. In this Hanael is often called 'the Angel of the Innocents and Hope', to remind us that we are the breath and will of God, particularly when we beseech thus:

Enchanting And Invoking God's Warrior:

Dear Archangel Hanael,

Please assist me with your Warrior's strength to enlighten my path when I am straying from certainty.

Please enchant me to steadfastly achieve positive and constructive purpose, for the joy of life, so that I may uplift the journey of my brothers and sisters.

Please show me the clarity of my destiny, and stop me from wavering in strength from my life's path.

ELEEMOMKA

So be it.

Amen.

JOPHIEL
Sacred Name: **Sacred Liberator**
Divine Action: **The Beauty of God**
Colour Ray: **Yellow**
Mineral Stone: **Citrine**
Essence: **Narcissus**

Jophiel is commanded from the Source to tend the beauty of our Planetary home, the Blue Planet. Earth is called thus, because the landmass of its sphere is 70% water, and from outer space shines as an exquisite azure blue. The water of our Globe allows the current and vibration of feeling to fully flow, and at present the water molecule in our body is expanding through the work of Jophiel.

See Professor Mazuru Emoto's *Miracles in Water,* who stirs us with information about the power of water. This is inspired by Jophiel, who also tends to the function of the creative presence, and all its liberty emerging through the joy of the arts, and the creation of beauty, as an emanation of the Divine. Jophiel brings freshness and liberation to enchant life into pleasure, and to bring the illumination of the soul. So if you need to discern and remove clutter from your home or life, ask Jophiel to help you thus:

Enchanting And Invoking God's Provider Of Beauty:

Dear Archangel Jophiel,
Please help me to discern the beauty and pleasure of creation living through me.
Please help me to hear your heralding call in order to receive your Divine liberation, and play.
Please allow your powerful wisdom to uplift me and carry me to that space of inspiration in the now-ness of now, which I know will take me to the beauty of my Divine service.
ELEEMOMKA
So be it.
Amen.

METATRON
Sacred Name: **The Lustrous Teacher**
Divine Action: **Angel of the Presence**
Colour Ray: **White/Silver**
Mineral Stone: **Clear Quartz**
Essence: **Frankincense**

Metatron gives counsel to us as a lustrous teacher, and is often referred to as the voice of God. When calling his name, be prepared for a lightning flash which will ask you to step up your spiritual practice, to improve your choices by reaffirming Love, Patience and Unity, throughout every aspect of your life.

Metatron literally sees through our incarnation, and this is why we feel both held by this Archangel's love and urged further. All our choices, all our thoughts make up the shape of our destiny, and so Metatron encourages us to be precise and present with each decision, so as to not create future karma.

Metatron is the keeper of the Akashic Hall of Records, the Universal Book of Life, the Cosmic Library of the Mind of God, and so there is no thought, word or deed that misses the attention of this great Archangel. In essence this merciful Teacher is completely in tune with divine and cosmic intelligence, producing wisdom through miracles. Therefore, listening to Metatron's wise voice will lead you to the true direction of your heart and soul's attainment.

Metatron was once the Prophet Enoch, who was so rich in virtue that the Infinite One compelled Enoch to become an Archangel. In that moment Enoch the man was consumed by the element of fire and passed into the kingdom of God to sit on the right side of the supreme Throne.

Evoking Metatron's energy fires through any surfeit, any 'energy holding' or barrier that stops you from seeing the truth, and therefore call the Angel thus:

Enchanting And Invoking God's Lustrous Teacher:

Dear Archangel Metatron,
Please allow me to dedicate my life to the path of initiation that beholds my soul full of light.
Please teach me to transform my actions by your all-seeing presence and wisdom, transmuting all to the highest choice.
I surrender myself to the illumination of the only path of truth, to live and breathe each action as a reflection of the Divine.

ELEEMOMKA
So be it.
Amen.

MICHAEL
Sacred Name: **The Divine Leader**
Divine Action: **One who is with God**
Colour Ray: **Violet**
Mineral Stone: **Amethyst**
Essence: **Rose**

Michael provides unequivocal information about our soul's mission in the Divine Plan. Therefore, if we are ever lost or uncertain and we beseech the help of Michael, direct action always arrives as loving guidance. In this we are reminded that the heart is the treasure store of all knowing, and that it is only the incoherence of confused thought that takes us from our path.

Once we are encouraged back onto the path of our own unique destiny, this exquisite Archangel moves us to be the master/mistress of our lives through the I AM Presence. When Michael is by your side you will feel no fear or uncertainty. Rather you will experience enchantment and the ability to transmute any challenge.

See this magnificent Archangel with a sword of Truth, a shield of Virtue and a crown of God's Light. For Michael is the Angel of true leadership, and so takes us into the kingdom of creativity.

Enchanting And Invoking God's Brilliant Angelic Leader:

Dear Archangel Michael,
Please fill me from the brow to the toe with your celestial light, allowing me to see my soul's core and shape my destiny.
Help me to take charge of my spiritual growth, and to be the commander of my own frequency as life unfolds.
Please purify my attention to see the constant flame of the divine light within me, so that my being is always honed by unconditional love.
ELEEMOMKA
So be it.
Amen.

RAZIEL

Sacred Name: **The Keeper of the Mysteries**
Divine Action: **The secrets of God**
Colour Ray: **Indigo**
Mineral Stone: **Obsidian**
Essence: **Violet**

Raziel's Archangelic splendour is derived from sitting extremely close to God. In this position all the information about the mysteries of the Cosmos are heard.

There is an ancient legend, which speaks of God giving Raziel a Book of Knowledge that informed Adam about the spiritual laws of creation, the nature of life, and the ability to speak the essence of the word, the great OM. Therefore, Raziel is chiefly associated with arousing within us that part we play in the unfolding nature of creation, as the mystery of the Divine is revealed within us.

Raziel is an extraordinarily wise teacher, administering to us through our intuition or secrets, and is most alert in us during times of retreat, or when we are dreaming.

Whoever seeks the Divine finds that the experience does not come from the mental body alone, but from the very depths of the soul. This creates God-consciousness within us. Therefore, Raziel oversees the secret chamber of the heart, knowing that when we choose to enter, veils of illusion are parted, and what is revealed defies the rational mind, suffusing science with conscience. For knowing the conditions of life is contained in science, whereas knowing the condition of the after-life develops the art of conscience.

Raziel asks us to pledge that all experience associated with the mysteries be given for the furtherance of truth in God, and the glory of all, rather than for personal gain. From this position we may truly cultivate the faithful aspect of our consciousness.

Enchanting And Invoking God's Teacher of Secrets:

Dear Archangel Raziel,
Please show me the elixir of your divine insight, and purify my intuition with the wisdom of creation filled with beauty.
Please shine light on the mystery of my life, so that full awareness dawns, releasing karma and urging my love to embrace my role as a servant of creation.

Allow me to know this 'truth' in the deepest part of my soul and body, so that I may carry the light within me wherever I may be.

Teach me to not stumble on my path, and remain woven within the conviction of the divine matrix, which is supreme love.

ELEEMOMKA

So be it.

Amen.

RAPHAEL

Sacred Name: **The Loving Healer**

Divine Action: **God healed**

Colour Ray: **Green**

Mineral Stone: **Emerald**

Essence: **Lavender**

The beauty and bounty of Raphael is the healing and comfort that emerges from the multitudinous rays that shine from the body of this exquisite Archangel.

Healing means " moving back to wholeness", and so when we seek Raphael's warm alchemy, we are taken to that supreme space within us, where 'All Is Well', where all negativity is transformed.

Raphael is the healer of the earth, a notion revealed in the Law of the Zohar; an ancient Rabbinical text known as the Book of Splendour. Raphael is reputed to have given Noah a Book of Medicine to be taken on his epic voyage within the Ark.

Therefore, when we beseech Raphael for healing, and we are healed, Raphael emits the inspiration of care for our planet, and encourages us to create communion with our earthy nature. Healing in this sense means that when we cleanse ourselves, we grow through the new cycles of evolution, both in our life, and the life of our Planet Earth. In this regard, this great Angel teaches us empathy.

Enchanting And Invoking God's Healer:

Dear Archangel Raphael,

I ask you for the manna of Divine Love that flows through you from the Infinite One.

May you bless me with faith, mercy and truth, and allow me to be a conduit for divine healing, so that I may serve the inspiration of the collective.

May you teach me ways of steadfast loving when faced with the negativity of my own shadow, or the shadow of my brothers and sisters, so that I transform all and become a vessel of God's love.
ELEEMOMKA
So be it.
Amen.

SANDALPHON
Sacred Name: **The Divine Guardian**
Divine Action: **Sacred Brother**
Colour Ray: **Brown**
Mineral Stone: **Amber**
Essence: **Sandalwood**

Sandalphon is God's Guardian vibration here on Earth, the kingdom of creative purpose, where thought creates the energy of our inner and outer worlds. This great Angel of the Earth considers the cycles of nature within his gaze, and therefore stands in the material world holding the torch of conviction for the Divine meeting the profane; this force holds the vibration of co-creativity.

Sandalphon is also the Angel Patron of Music, allowing the Divine to pour through the vibration of musical harmony, particularly in the music that is given to the sacred.

Ancient legends suggest that Sandalphon was the prophet Elijah before being elevated to the Archangel kingdoms, and Jewish Law suggests Elijah still walks on Earth reforming our search for the Divine.

Enchanting And Evoking God's Supernal Guardian:

Dear Archangel Sandalphon,
Thank you for blessing the world of nature and all the elemental forces here on Earth.
Please bring me into the harmony of balanced accord, enlightening my service to creation, and putting my trust in the substance of surrendering to the natural cycles of life.
Please allow me to connect with the vibration of balance between my material and spiritual life.
ELEEMOMKA
So be it.
Amen.

SHAMAEL
Sacred Name: **The Sacred Guide**
Divine Action: **The One who seeks God**
Colour Ray: **Lilac**
Mineral Stone: **Mother Of Pearl**
Essence: **Hyacinth**

Shamael, sometimes spelt Samael and sometimes Chamuel, is the Archangel that administers to the core principles of life, helping us to become clearly focused.

Shamael is often reputed to be the Archangel who gave succour to Jesus in the Garden of Gethsemane.

Archangel healing on this specific level occurs by the removal of any negative bonding within the material aspect of our lives. When this occurs, all negativity is erased from our life; all the baggage that prevents us from seeing the true path that spiritual discipline provides.

Shamael is particularly useful to us during times of great change such as Divorce or Bereavement, helping us to pare away the superfluities of life, and to release the attachment to sentimentality. In so doing we are encouraged to remove those aspects of our lives that diminish our belief in the Divine, and merely attach us to possessions which create a compound feeling of loss, rather than allowing us to meet the spirit of adventure, and letting our spirits soar. Therefore, this divine guide is often seen as the Angel of creativity or new beginnings. Shamael encourages serene and beauteous living.

Enchanting And Invoking God's Guiding Principle:

Dear Archangel Shamael,
Please help me to fully comprehend the teaching of change and the wisdom of uncertainty, particularly when I am tested by its presence.
Please let me see how adversity leads to abundance, and show me how wisdom shines when chaos leads to coherence.
Please direct me to administer my affairs on the true path, so that I do not become caught by the illusions of the material world.
ELEEMOMKA
So be it.
Amen.

URIEL
Sacred Name: **The Divine Companion**
Divine Action: **God is Light**
Colour Ray: **Pink**
Mineral Stone: **Pink Quartz**
Essence: **Rosemary**

Uriel is sometimes written as, Ouriel, Auriel or Ariel, and is the Angel of Destiny, fully knowing the secrets of our pathway through the folds of time-past and time-future.

Uriel maintains a powerful link with the knowledge of existence, shining light on our path as we stumble forward, and calling our souls back into our bodies if we choose to let them leave through adversity, ill health, or imbalanced behaviour.

Archangelic light becomes Uriel as the great companion, because all our dreams or visions of a psychic nature can be illuminated by this Angels truth in acts that fulfil our creativity, bravery, kindness and love. This Angel's catchphrase is: "In freedom there lies abundance, and in friendship there lies trust."

Enchanting And Invoking God's Companion Of Light:

Dear Archangel Uriel,

As you are placed in the role of a stabilizing presence on the Earth, please watch over me, so that I may tread the path of gentleness and care.

Please teach me to be in the world but not of it, allowing my spiritual gifts to unfold, as well as moving my material life into abundance.

I am destiny's child and so please show me the path of joy, through which the way of love will fully manifest.

ELEEMOMKA

So be it.

Amen.

ZADKIEL
Sacred Name: **The Great Comforter**
Divine Action: **The Righteousness of God**
Colour Ray: **Turquoise**
Mineral Stone: **Larimar**
Essence: **Sage**

Zadkiel provides divine comfort, fortifying our lives with a wealth of instruction, and shielding us from the demons, or projections of our fears. This wisdom will allow us to see that any obstacle to our spiritual and material abundance is perpetuated by self-limiting belief. Zadkiel shows us what needs to be healed and brought forth into the light.

Zadkiel teaches us to open our hearts and to reveal our generosity and kindness to others, particularly when the quest for material comfort has been successfully gained. You see working with Zadkiel means a continuous flow of treasure supported by Divine love, and derived from the supporting exercise of belief, faith and trust. The Source is a place of complete well-being, untroubled by issues of scarcity, so there is no budgeting needed, only belief in the splendour of love; reminding us of our need to be grateful for the gifts of life.

Enchanting And Invoking The Holy Comforter:

Dear Archangel Zadkiel,
Thank you for the comfort and abundance of the Divine succour that you have revealed to me.
Please allow me to breathe the pure light of the immortal Prana-yama, so that my vitality and strength may uplift the lives of my fellow earth beings.
As you journey through our lives, please awaken within us the glory of our gratitude for the great gifts of the spirit.
ELEEMOMKA
So be it.
Amen.

ZAPHKIEL
Sacred Name: **The Divine Lover**
Divine Action: **The Compassionate Embrace**
Colour Ray: **Orange**
Mineral Stone: **Carnelian**
Essence: **Cinnamon**

Zaphkiel is often known as Cassiel, and is an agent of grace holding us in true compassion. Often this Archangel is seen in solitude, moving through the vale of tears that the weary, sad, and lost ones move through, always touching all with no effort but the warm caress of one who knows, and therefore offering mercy.

When we feel alone and in desolation, Zaphkiel always appears at our behest, reminding us of the love that rays from the Source, and that we have forgotten. Therefore, this Angel of Love encourages us to find romance in our life, surrendering to the ecstasy of true passion.

Anxiety always precedes change, and so if we can open our hearts and yield to these moments, we can be amazed by what flows through to us - such tenderness, such grace.

Enchanting And Invoking The Divine Lover:

> *Dear Archangel Zaphkiel,*
> *Please hold me in this moment, and allow me your gracious touch, so that I may pledge myself to heal through loving.*
> *Please see me as one who passionately seeks the passion of compassion, so that I may surrender to the greatness of passion and love.*
> *Allow me the possibility of rising through grace to a richer sunset, so that I may once again marvel in the glory of the Source feeling the ecstasy of nature upon me.*
> *ELEEMOMKA*
> *So be it.*
> *Amen.*

Many of my clients have been visited by the Heart Angels as I work with the Divine Sona or Sound, and I'm often reminded of a few lines of a favourite poem by Samuel Taylor Coleridge, which describes the awe-inspiring presence of these fire-filled Guardians of Light. I've added a few personal changes to make sense of the many from the one:

"And all who heard should see them there,

And all should cry "Beware, Beware!"
Their flashing eyes, their floating hair!
Weave a circle round them thrice,
And close your eyes with holy dread,
For they on honey dew hath fed,
And drunk the milk of Paradise."

Angels Of Atlantis Meditation

- Move to your sacred space and make sure that you won't be disturbed. Ring a bell, burn a candle and incense, and make sure voicemail is on. Regard the space as peace-filled as possible.
- Find a position in which your body feels aligned and full of weight; this may be lying down in supine, sitting cross-legged on the floor, or upright in a chair. The important thing is that you feel your spine's pranic cord open and aligned. Free up any tensions in your neck or shoulders just by rotating them or lifting them up and then releasing them.
- As you compose yourself, use a mudra for your fingers, bringing the tip of your thumb and forefinger together connecting the sun and moon elements within your energy field. Or, bring each finger together fanning your hands into an open pattern, which brings all of the major planets together into your soul system.
- Breathe in deeply three times, seeing the breath as light filling your body, and not rushing the breath but by feeling a deeper and deeper calm moving through the whole of your being.
- Visualize the breath-light seeping through the whole of you, and as you finish the third wide-deep breath. See the pranic cord of light through the whole of your spine: take the light deep down into the floor of the building, then moving down through the levels of soil, clay, stone and rock, until you reach bedrock in the very womb of Mother Earth ~ then rest for a few moments.
- Breathe in deeply three times, feeling your body yield to the sublime unconditional love of the Divine Mother, the Gaia. If you wish, ask Mother for a gift, a sign, or a vision. Then, with thanks in your heart, siphon the energy up through the pranic cord, up from the levels of the deep earth until you reach the middle of your torso around your heart chakra.
- Allow the gifts from Mother Earth to be placed in your Heart's Secret Chamber (see this as a beautiful Quartz Crystal Cave), and then continue with the Pranic Cord moving upwards through your spine, and

- out through the top of your head, through the building in which you are placed into planetary space, and then outer space.
- At this point, feel where your own planetary home may be, beyond this Blue Planet. If unsure, simply connect with the planet Venus, which is the planet of love. Then let your pranic cord connect with her planetary source. Pause, breathing in three times, in and out, the wonderful energy of the soul-ar system. This cording is vitally important for the journey we are about to begin.
- Then came back into the centre of your torso, rest in the Heart Chakra for a moment, and see the Crystal Cave of your Heart's Secret Chamber.
- Then sound **OM** three times.
- As a sonic talisman, this will open the door to the chamber of your heart. See the door opening and walk into your chamber.
- Before you, see a beautifully round Quartz Crystal Cave with the Twelve Archangels sitting in alcoves within the walls of the cave. Each cove or niche will be lined with the mineral stone dedicated to the Divine action of each Archangel:
  - Gabriel the Messenger sitting in a Lapis Lazuli alcove
  - Hanael the Warrior within Ruby.
  - Jophiel the Liberator within Citrine.
  - Metatron the great Teacher in a Diamond alcove.
  - Michael the Leader in Amethyst.
  - Raziel the Mystery Keeper in Iolite.
  - Raphael the Healer within Emerald.
  - Sandalphon the Guardian in Amber.
  - Shamael the Guide in Moonstone.
  - Uriel the Companion in Pink Quartz.
  - Zadkiel the Comforter in Larimar.
  - Zaphkiel the Lover within Carnelian.
- **PAUSE:** Breathe in the Divine elixir of their multi-dimensional energies and sound **OM** three times, thanking the Archangels for this unique celestial visit to the Secret Chamber of the heart.
- In front of each Angel you will see a beautiful bejewelled casket, and within each casket will be a proverb teaching, an oracular statement to provide you with guidance. Move to the centre of the cave and sit on the violet cushioned chair that is placed before you in the centre of the room. This will be your meditating throne to receive the special energies of the Archangelic treasured counsel, all through the pure vibration of feeling.

- **PAUSE**: Breathe in three times the exquisite elixir of the Angels breath. This is fifth/seventh dimensional ether and needs time to be absorbed. It is an Alchemical Gift from the Violet Flame and will utterly transform your state. Feel this drawn through the whole of your being whilst guidance soars in your soul and prepares you for a special gift from each of the Archangels.
- You will possibly be aware of many impressions such as dancing lights moving through your mental body, or powerful intuitive insights, like laser feelings of healing, or in this extraordinary Secret Chamber of your Heart, an oracular message of awesome magnitude.
- Listen to the inner calling of your heart, dowse with your heart, breathe in the pulse of your heart, and as you perceive this vital information, decide which Archangelic casket draws your attention most for this particular sitting. (There will be further sittings for other meditations on future days)
- See the luminescent rays shining from each Archangelic alcove:

  - Gabriel ~ Blue
  - Hanael ~ Red
  - Jophiel ~ Yellow
  - Metatron ~ Silver White
  - Michael ~ Violet
  - Raziel ~ Indigo
  - Raphael ~ Green
  - Sandalphon ~ Amber
  - Shamael ~Lilac
  - Uriel ~ Pink
  - Zadkiel ~ Turquoise
  - Zaphkiel ~ Orange

- When you have chosen the casket, telepathically communicate to the Archangelic presence what your choice is, and observe how the casket is opened by a Faery presence. As the casket opens, you will hear tones move through the air towards you. They are the Celestial Sona of this gift.
- See the beautiful Light that shines forth from the casket. Both Sound and Light (the Divine elements of Transformation and Information) carry with them the proverb's teaching into your force, into your heart's chamber. Once there, you will turn its vibration into your own note's truth ~ a key for each 'treasure counsel' appears at the end of this book.

EPILOGUE

Knowing ourselves truly is the only way. When our minds are full of illumination, when the word is made flesh, when our hearts are full of love, and our bodies are filled with the flow of the universe, the harmony of this knowledge resounds and echoes throughout our whole being, the whole planet and the Cosmos. Harmony is both of this world and not of this world. Harmony as the light of life helps us to elevate our consciousness, when once more we are drawn to cure by love, the conceit, the lies and the treachery of our shadow.

Wholeheartedly I believe that harmony, as an agency of God's creation, brings integration to the mind and body, and therefore to heaven and the Earth. Harmony is our source and our destiny, and my writing has attempted to weave this within a tapestry that tells the epic story occurring at this time. Now as we move through this stage of the adventure of life, we are daring to recognise we are not what we were, but becoming something that is both emotionally mature and spiritually richer. At least I hope so.

Our evolution is to ride the current crises of our changing world, and transform both life on earth and in ourselves through the acknowledgement and experience of the Heart's love, as a divining chamber for God's love. If we can love as God loves, help as God helps, give as God gives, serve as God serves, be with God, then we cease longing for the light of heaven, because heaven is ours now, then, and always. The light of heaven always cracks open our mind, for we are intended to live the light that casts out the darkness of our lives.

To begin with we need only two simple steps, that of living Grace and Truth, for they are concomitant with the light of the Love that is the heavenly harmony of the Angels. When we truly vibrate these virtues, our heart quivers with the song of our soul, because this is what it was created for. When we mature in this way, the beauty of our youth steals inwards, making us more magnetic. And so with this time of bloom, we find our hearts in hiding, stirred by the beauty of the harmony and the light, making us wiser.

As we accept our hearts as the locus of life, the entire richness of life begins to furrow inwards, deep into our muscles and bones, way into the invisible realms, and of course magic is borne of the invisible planes.

The great magic that fountains forth at this time is the meeting point between the quantum mind and the three-dimensional mind, and that by our striving to purity, we may just change our cellular being into the evolution of a triple helix DNA, and so we radiate greater light. Now, through these efforts and in good time, we too are called to a powerfully new and greater vision: that if we think thoughts filled with love, we may just bring about a world that is full of peace.

It is not until we think thoughts of peace, that peace in our hearts will reign. It is not until we believe that conflict is impossible, that the light will prevail. Then we will not end war because we hate it, but because we love peace infinitely more. If and only if we can live this love in our hearts, one day we will notice that all conflict has disappeared, because we know and say as the great Hawaiian Kahuna:

I love you, please forgive me, I'm sorry, Thank you!

This is the time in all our lives to reach deep into the library of life, and to heal those aspects of self that are held in the folds of the book of life, those parts of ourselves that are hidden in the shadows of the print, or covered with the dust of wretchedness.

This is the time to make a radical change to those weaker parts of self, devoting each moment to the elimination of that part of our psyche that tends towards ruin. This cannot be done without work, this cannot be made without help, this cannot be achieved without gracious honesty and the power of devoted chant and prayer. But when it is done, we may just achieve the illumination of self-mastery, feeling our skin shine the light of the resurrected ones.

Imagine yourself as the illumined being you wish to be. See yourself fully gaining the humility, insight and kindness that it takes to become a beacon of light. Our world needs spiritual genius and might, for nothing can be gained by playing safe because we believe that safety lies in so doing.

Imagine all of your weakness transformed into strength, see yourself beautiful, calm and wise, and don't refuse yourself anything. Ask the Angels to bring the spirit of the Source into you, so that you can give birth to the newness of you, repairing your soul and loving the incandescent nature of your shining presence. So that when you move back into the darker aspects of the world, you take the brilliance of you with you, and spread the light of the heavenly kingdom throughout.

Remember that in any given situation you can shine this brightly because gratitude is in your heart, love is in your soul. When we bring this to the fore, when we bring the love of the Source through us and bless all things, we are surrounded by spiritual ecstasy. Then and most mercifully only then, you will move in co-creation with the Divine, and together you will change the world.

"If there is righteousness in the heart,
There will be beauty in the character.
If there is beauty in the character,
There will be harmony in the home.
If there is harmony in the home,
There will be order in the nation.
If there is order in the nation,
There will be peace within the world."
- CONFUCIUS

KEYS FOR THE
ANGELIC CASKETS

GABRIEL ~ THE MESSAGE OF INSPIRATION

Inspirational enchantment is moving fully into your life. The joy and awe of innocence are the gatekeepers of this treasure. Seek out these elements, and the law of attraction will spin a spell of magic for you.

HANAEL ~ THE MESSAGE OF STRENGTH

Seek out your strength; its courage, hope and truth will succour you. Hope nourishes the soul and encourages our hearts to respond in like mind.

JOPHIEL ~ THE MESSAGE OF PLAYFULNESS

Live the vitality and zest of each moment. Decide to include an activity in your daily schedule that draws you to the playfulness of your inner child. Also, think about ways in which you can increase play in your daily living.

METATRON ~ THE MESSAGE OF MERCY & FORGIVENESS

Is there someone you need to forgive, or perhaps it's yourself? When you forgive, your heart will brim with mercy and love, as forgiveness is the key to heaven. Forgiveness allows our hearts to grow in dimension as love emerges to replace the pain of the test.

MICHAEL ~ THE MESSAGE IS PATIENCE

Bring patience back into your life. You have been doing too much, whether this be over-working or over-playing your energies. Give yourself time for recovery and meditation. Ground yourself daily through breath and sound techniques, so that you feel equilibrium during each of your days.

RAZIEL ~ THE MESSAGE OF SPIRITUAL GROWTH

It is time to consider the spiritual aspect of your life. Perhaps this is because of challenge and change. Try to spend a few moments a day meditating, giving love or gracious energy to a loved one, a friend or colleague, a passer-by, or tending the beauty of the natural world.

RAPHAEL ~THE MESSAGE OF PHYSICAL HEALTH

Your health needs careful management. Take time for Sound Healing, Crystal Therapy, Massage, Reflexology, Reiki, or a treatment founded in the healing touch. Conversely, this could be an Archangelic praise of how you are loved for loving your body through a positive health regime.

SANDALPHON ~ THE MESSAGE OF ABUNDANCE

There is abundance occurring on your path, and much joy will be had. Prepare yourself by enjoying a rampage of appreciation for the gifts you have, and create space for receiving even more love and more joy. The universe is rich with joy as the derivation of Source energy, that All is Well.

SHAMAEL ~ THE MESSAGE OF TRANSFORMATION

A new project, a new friendship, or a new happening is coming your way. This is a time when your patient visualizing brings forth fruit, when your dreams become material realities, and you transform. Move into love and all will manifest!

URIEL ~ THE MESSAGE OF MEDITATION

Meditation will allow you to hear the thoughts of God, and so take time to be fully vigilant of this practice. If you are already meditating, attempt a subtle change in your regime to embrace an even deeper vibrational harmonic of the "holy whole."

ZADKIEL ~ THE MESSAGE OF RETREAT

Be comforted by the notion of a quiet retreat. Take time to be still and simply 'be'. This is a time for reflection, for re-evaluating a situation, and for perceiving resolution and atonement as healing.

ZAPHKIEL ~ THE MESSAGE OF ROMANCE

Love is in the air. New love is awaiting you, or maybe it is a new way of loving your current lover or beloved. The observation of romance is something that will infuse your life with joy ~ watch a romantic film, read a romantic novel, listen to romantic music, gaze at a natural landscape of renowned romantic beauty. Dream of an occasion when you can bring romance into your life, or remember the feelings of a blissful experience.

FINDHORN PRESS

Life Changing Books

For a complete catalogue,
please contact:

Findhorn Press Ltd
117-121 High Street,
Forres IV36 1AB,
Scotland, UK

t +44 (0)1309 690582
f +44 (0)131 777 2711
e info@findhornpress.com

or consult our catalogue online
(with secure order facility) on
www.findhornpress.com

For information on the Findhorn Foundation:
www.findhorn.org